Penny Stocks to Multibagger

The Complete Guide to Finding Hidden Gems, Building Wealth, and Turning Small Investments into Massive Returns

Deepanshu Suman

2025 First Edition

Copyright

Title: Penny Stocks to Multibagger
Author: Deepanshu Suman

First Edition
ISBN: 978-93-344-5629-5

Disclaimer: This book is intended for educational and informational purposes only. It presents strategies, concepts, and frameworks related to penny stocks, trading, and investment. It does not constitute financial, legal, or professional advice. Readers should conduct their own research and consult qualified professionals before making investment decisions.

Dedication

To all aspiring investors and lifelong learners,
who dare to dream big and take the first step,
this book is for you.

Acknowledgments

I would like to express my deepest gratitude to everyone who contributed to the creation of this book:

- My mentors and teachers, whose guidance shaped my understanding of finance and investing.
- Fellow traders and investors, for sharing insights and experiences that inspired the case studies in this book.
- Family and friends, for their unwavering support and patience throughout this journey.
- The authors, researchers, and analysts whose work laid the foundation for modern investment strategies.

Finally, I thank my readers. Your curiosity, ambition, and willingness to learn are the true drivers behind this work.

Preface

Investing in penny stocks can feel like a high-stakes gamble, but behind the risk lies the potential for extraordinary wealth. Over the years, I have studied markets across India, the US, and emerging economies, observing patterns, successes, and failures. This book was written to help you navigate that world with clarity, discipline, and a systematic approach.

My goal is not to promise quick riches. Instead, I aim to equip you with the knowledge, tools, and frameworks to make informed decisions, manage risk, and identify high-potential opportunities. You will find practical exercises, real-world case studies, and actionable strategies that can transform small investments into long-term wealth.

Whether you are a beginner taking your first steps in the market or an experienced trader looking to refine your approach, this book will guide you through a step-by-step journey. Think of it as your roadmap—from small investments today to multibagger returns tomorrow.

Let this book be your companion on the path to financial growth, helping you build not just wealth, but the confidence and systems to sustain it over a lifetime.

Introduction

Investing is not just a set of transactions—it is a **mindset**. The **Multibagger Mindset** is the ability to identify opportunities where small, carefully chosen investments can grow exponentially over time. This book is designed to help you cultivate that mindset, equipping you with the **knowledge, strategies, and tools** to navigate the high-risk yet highly rewarding world of penny stocks and small-cap investments.

Why This Book Exists

Penny stocks are often misunderstood. Some see them as pure speculation or dangerous gambles, while others view them as a shortcut to wealth. The truth is nuanced: **penny stocks are both high-risk and highly transformative.**

This book exists to:

- **Unlock the power of compounding:** Discover how even small investments, when applied strategically, can accumulate into life-changing wealth over time.
- **Demystify risk and reward:** Understand the volatility inherent in penny stocks, and learn how to separate high-potential opportunities from reckless gambles.
- **Provide a global perspective:** Explore insights and strategies relevant to India, the US, and other emerging markets, giving you a broader, more informed view of opportunities.
- **Teach systematic investing:** Move beyond luck or guesswork. Build a **repeatable, step-by-step framework** for long-term wealth creation.

Who This Book Is For

This guide is written for anyone who wants to approach investing with **clarity, structure, and discipline**:

- **Beginners** seeking structured, step-by-step learning to confidently enter the market.
- **Traders** aiming for explosive returns while managing calculated risk.
- **Long-term investors** focused on multibagger opportunities and sustainable portfolio growth.
- **Anyone** who wants actionable strategies and practical guidance, instead of vague tips or unverified advice.

How to Use This Book

To maximize your results:

- **Follow the progression:** Start with foundational concepts and move gradually toward advanced strategies. Each chapter builds on the last to create a coherent investing framework.
- **Apply what you learn:** Use exercises, worksheets, and real-world case studies to practice and reinforce concepts.
- **Analyze examples:** Learn from historical successes and failures to sharpen your judgment and avoid common mistakes.
- **Build your own system:** Leverage the frameworks, tools, and checklists in this book to create a **personalized, repeatable process** for identifying high-potential multibaggers.

By actively engaging with this book, you will develop a mindset that not only identifies profitable opportunities but also **manages risk intelligently**, empowering you to pursue long-term wealth creation with confidence, discipline, and clarity.

Contents

Part I

Penny Stocks Fundamentals

Chapter 1

Penny Stocks Demystified

Penny stocks are often shrouded in mystery and misconception. For some, they represent the ultimate high-risk gamble; for others, a hidden path to extraordinary wealth. In this chapter, we will break down the myths, define what penny stocks are across different markets, and explain how they differ from other types of equities.

You will learn the definitions used in India, the US, and global markets, providing a clear framework for understanding which stocks qualify as "penny" and why they exist. We will explore their history, tracing their evolution from over-the-counter (OTC) markets to modern exchanges like Nasdaq and NSE, and uncover how regulation, market structure, and investor behavior have shaped them.

Furthermore, we will address common myths and misconceptions—are penny stocks scams? Are they legal? Can they be ethically invested in? By separating fact from fiction, you will gain the confidence to navigate this unique segment of the stock market with clarity.

Finally, this chapter compares penny stocks with micro-cap, small-cap, and blue-chip stocks. Understanding these distinctions will allow you to see why multibagger opportunities are often concentrated in smaller, less-followed companies, and why these investments, while riskier, offer the potential for exceptional returns.

By the end of this chapter, you will have a **solid foundation and a clear understanding of penny stocks**, setting the stage for deeper exploration of analysis, strategy, and real-world application in the chapters ahead.

1.1 What Are Penny Stocks?

Penny stocks are one of the most intriguing yet misunderstood segments of the financial markets. Simply put, they are shares of small companies that trade at a relatively low price per share. While the exact threshold varies from market to market, the essence remains the same: these are **afford-**

able, high-risk, high-reward investments that operate largely outside the mainstream spotlight.

Unlike well-known blue-chip companies that dominate headlines and analyst reports, penny stocks often exist in the shadows. They are small-cap or micro-cap companies—sometimes startups, sometimes older businesses that haven't yet scaled. Because of their size and low share price, these stocks are highly volatile, capable of making large gains or losses in very short periods. This volatility, combined with their affordability, is what draws ambitious investors seeking the possibility of a "multibagger" return—an investment that multiplies many times over.

The Core Characteristics of Penny Stocks

Across markets worldwide, penny stocks share several defining traits:

- **Low price per share:** Typically, these shares are priced far below mainstream stocks, making them accessible to investors with modest capital.
- **Small market capitalization:** Penny stock companies usually have a smaller total value, meaning they have not yet reached the scale or stability of established large-cap firms.
- **Limited liquidity:** Fewer buyers and sellers trade these stocks regularly, which can lead to wide bid-ask spreads and sudden price swings.
- **High volatility and growth potential:** Small size and low price make these stocks highly sensitive to market news, company developments, or investor sentiment.
- **Minimal analyst coverage:** Many penny stocks operate under the radar, with little media attention or research reports. This lack of coverage makes due diligence essential.

These characteristics combine to create an environment where significant profits—and equally significant losses—are possible. Investors are drawn to penny stocks for the potential of **exponential growth**, but the risk is real and must be carefully managed.

Penny Stocks in a Global Context

While specific definitions and regulatory guidelines differ across countries, the general concept of penny stocks exists globally. In the United States, for example, the Securities and Exchange Commission (SEC) often classifies stocks below $5 that trade outside major exchanges as penny stocks. In India, shares trading at relatively low prices, often under INR 10 20, are considered penny stocks. Across Europe, Southeast Asia, Africa, and Latin

America, low-priced shares with similar traits exist on smaller exchanges or over-the-counter platforms.

Regardless of geography, the principles are consistent: these stocks are small, under-followed, volatile, and potentially transformative for disciplined investors. However, the degree of regulation, transparency, and liquidity may differ widely depending on the market, which adds another layer of complexity for global investors.

Why Penny Stocks Matter

Understanding penny stocks is more than an academic exercise—it is the first step toward harnessing their potential. These stocks represent the **frontier of opportunity**: a place where careful analysis, strategic timing, and disciplined risk management can transform small investments into life-changing wealth. Unlike mainstream stocks, where returns are often steady and predictable, penny stocks offer the chance to achieve outsized gains—but only for those willing to approach them methodically.

By the end of this section, you should have a clear sense of what penny stocks are, what makes them different from other equities, and why they capture the attention of ambitious investors worldwide. With this foundational understanding, you are now ready to explore their history, behavior, and strategies in the chapters that follow.

History: From OTC Markets to Modern Exchanges

The story of penny stocks is intertwined with the evolution of financial markets themselves. To understand why penny stocks exist, how they operate, and why they can offer both extraordinary opportunity and high risk, it is essential to look at their history—from humble over-the-counter (OTC) beginnings to their presence on modern exchanges like Nasdaq, NSE, and beyond.

The Origins: Over-the-Counter (OTC) Markets

In the earliest days of financial markets, not all companies were listed on formal exchanges. Small companies and startups often issued shares directly to investors or traded them through informal networks. This system, known as the **over-the-counter (OTC) market**, was decentralized, loosely regulated, and often opaque.

OTC markets provided a platform for companies that were too small, too new, or too risky to meet the stringent listing requirements of major exchanges. Investors in these markets were drawn by the possibility of **high returns from undervalued or emerging companies**, but they also faced significant risks, including lack of transparency, illiquidity, and the potential for manipulation.

Despite these challenges, OTC markets played a crucial role in **funding entrepreneurship and innovation**. They allowed companies to raise capital at an early stage, and they gave investors a chance to participate in growth stories before they became mainstream. Many successful companies today started life in OTC or secondary markets before graduating to larger exchanges.

Transition to Modern Exchanges

As financial systems matured, regulations evolved to protect investors while still allowing small companies access to capital. This evolution led to the creation of formal exchanges designed for low-priced and small-cap stocks. In the United States, for example, the **Nasdaq** became the home of many technology startups and smaller companies seeking liquidity and visibility. Nasdaq offered a **regulated, transparent, and electronic trading platform**, which significantly reduced the risks associated with OTC trading while opening up broader investor access.

In India, small-cap and penny stocks historically traded on the **Bombay Stock Exchange (BSE)** or over-the-counter networks before the establishment of the **National Stock Exchange (NSE)**. The NSE introduced electronic trading, real-time price discovery, and improved transparency, enabling investors to track small-cap stocks with greater confidence. These exchanges also provided regulatory oversight, helping reduce fraud and manipulation compared to earlier OTC practices.

Global Perspective

Globally, the evolution of penny stocks follows a similar trajectory: from informal, loosely regulated markets to formal exchanges that provide **liquidity, transparency, and accessibility**. In Europe, small-cap stocks often trade on regional exchanges with varying levels of oversight, while in emerging markets in Asia, Africa, and Latin America, local OTC or secondary markets still play an important role in early-stage investing.

The key takeaway is that regardless of geography, **penny stocks have always existed at the intersection of opportunity and risk**. They are the instruments through which small, innovative, or overlooked companies can raise capital and grow, while providing ambitious investors with a chance to capture outsized returns. The evolution of exchanges and regulation has reduced some risks, but the fundamental characteristics of penny stocks—volatility, low price, and potential for rapid growth—remain unchanged.

Why History Matters Today

Understanding this historical context is more than an academic exercise. It explains why penny stocks behave the way they do, why liquidity and volatility differ from large-cap stocks, and why investors must approach them with a disciplined, systematic strategy. From OTC networks where information was scarce and risk was high, to modern exchanges where technology and regulation have brought structure and transparency, penny stocks have always represented **a frontier of opportunity for informed and patient investors**.

By appreciating this history, you gain perspective on how penny stocks have evolved, why they exist, and how their unique characteristics can be leveraged to identify multibagger opportunities—without underestimating the risks involved.

Debunking Myths: Scams, Legality, and Ethical Investing

Penny stocks often carry a reputation that precedes them. In popular media and casual conversation, they are frequently labeled as "scams" or "get-rich-quick schemes." While it is true that penny stocks involve higher risk than mainstream investments, many of these perceptions are exaggerated or misunderstood. In this section, we will **debunk common myths**, clarify legal aspects, and explore how ethical investing applies in the penny stock universe.

Myth 1: Penny Stocks Are Always Scams

One of the most persistent myths is that all penny stocks are scams. This misconception arises because many small companies operate under less scrutiny than large-cap firms, and a few fraudulent actors have exploited these conditions in the past.

The reality: Penny stocks are *not inherently fraudulent.* They are simply shares of smaller, often under-followed companies that trade at low prices. The risks associated with penny stocks—such as high volatility, low liquidity, and limited public information—can sometimes be mistaken for scams. However, with proper research, due diligence, and risk management, penny stocks can be legitimate investment opportunities.

Myth 2: Penny Stocks Are Illegal

Another common myth is that buying and selling penny stocks is illegal or that these stocks exist outside the regulatory framework. This is false. In most countries, penny stocks are fully legal and regulated, although the rules governing them vary depending on the market.

For example:

- In the United States, the Securities and Exchange Commission (SEC) classifies penny stocks as shares trading below $5 and subject to specific disclosure and reporting rules.
- In India, the Securities and Exchange Board of India (SEBI) oversees small-cap and micro-cap stocks to ensure transparency and fair trading practices.
- Globally, every market has its own regulations defining legal thresholds, reporting requirements, and investor protections.

Understanding the regulatory environment is crucial. Investing in penny stocks is legal, but you must be aware of local laws, exchange rules, and reporting obligations to avoid unintentional violations.

Myth 3: Penny Stocks Are Unethical Investments

Some investors hesitate to invest in penny stocks because they believe doing so is unethical. This assumption often comes from stories of pump-and-dump schemes or manipulative trading. While unethical behavior does exist in certain corners of the market, the act of buying or selling penny stocks is not inherently unethical.

The reality: Ethical investing in penny stocks is entirely possible if you:

- Conduct thorough due diligence before investing.
- Avoid following hype or tips from unverified sources.
- Respect market rules and regulations.
- Focus on companies with transparent financials, honest management, and real business potential.

By approaching penny stocks with discipline and integrity, investors can participate in funding innovation, small businesses, and emerging markets, which contributes positively to the broader economy.

Separating Fact from Fiction

To navigate penny stocks safely, it is essential to separate myth from reality. Here are some practical tips:

- **Research is key:** Examine financial statements, promoter backgrounds, and company disclosures.
- **Avoid herd mentality:** Social media hype and unverified tips often amplify misconceptions.

- **Check regulatory filings:** Ensure the company complies with relevant authorities and exchange requirements.
- **Understand the risk:** Volatility and low liquidity are normal characteristics—not evidence of fraud.

Why Myths Persist

The myths surrounding penny stocks persist because of a combination of factors:

- **Media attention:** Headlines often focus on the few stories of extreme loss or fraud rather than the many legitimate investments.
- **Low barriers to entry:** Because anyone can invest with relatively little capital, inexperienced investors are more likely to be misled.
- **Historical frauds:** High-profile scams like pump-and-dump schemes have contributed to the negative reputation.

While awareness of these risks is critical, it should not discourage educated and disciplined investing. On the contrary, understanding the myths allows investors to navigate the market with confidence and identify genuine opportunities.

Key Takeaways

- Penny stocks are **not inherently scams or illegal**. They are small-cap stocks with unique characteristics.
- Ethical investing is possible and can even support innovation and growth in emerging businesses.
- Myths often exaggerate risk; informed investors can differentiate between speculation and fraud.
- Knowledge, research, and discipline are your most powerful tools for navigating the penny stock market successfully.

By debunking these myths, you are now better equipped to approach penny stocks with a clear, rational, and ethical mindset. This understanding forms the foundation for analyzing, selecting, and ultimately investing in penny stocks as part of a disciplined multibagger strategy.

Comparing Micro-Cap, Small-Cap, and Blue-Chip Markets

Investing in equities is not a one-size-fits-all endeavor. Stocks are often categorized by their **market capitalization**, which reflects the total value of a company's outstanding shares. Understanding the distinctions between micro-cap, small-cap, and blue-chip stocks is crucial for investors aiming to navigate the spectrum of risk, reward, and growth potential—especially when exploring penny stocks.

Micro-Cap Stocks: High Risk, High Potential

Micro-cap stocks represent the smallest publicly traded companies, typically with market capitalizations under $300 million (or the equivalent in other currencies). These companies are often young, niche, or emerging businesses with limited resources and visibility.

Characteristics:

- Extremely low stock prices, often classified as penny stocks.
- Limited liquidity, meaning buying or selling large quantities can significantly affect price.
- Sparse analyst coverage, which makes research more challenging but also creates opportunities for informed investors.
- High volatility: prices can swing dramatically on news, earnings, or market sentiment.

Why investors choose micro-caps: Micro-caps offer the potential for **exponential returns**. Because these companies are small, even modest growth in earnings or market share can lead to dramatic stock price appreciation. However, the risks are equally significant—financial instability, limited operational history, and susceptibility to market manipulation can result in substantial losses.

Small-Cap Stocks: Balancing Growth and Stability

Small-cap stocks generally have market capitalizations between $300 million and $2 billion. They are larger and more established than micro-caps but still offer higher growth potential than blue-chip companies.

Characteristics:

- Moderate stock prices compared to micro-caps.
- Greater liquidity, making trading easier without large price swings.
- More analyst coverage and public information available than micro-caps.
- Still volatile, but less extreme than micro-cap stocks.

Why investors choose small-caps: Small-cap stocks strike a **balance between growth and relative stability**. They can deliver strong returns as the companies expand, innovate, or capture niche markets, yet they are less prone to manipulation and extreme swings than micro-caps. Many successful multibagger stocks start as small-caps before becoming mid-cap or large-cap companies.

Blue-Chip Stocks: Stability and Predictability

Blue-chip stocks are shares of **large, established companies** with substantial market capitalization, often exceeding $10 billion. They are leaders in their industries and are typically characterized by stability, consistent earnings, and a history of dividend payments.

Characteristics:

- High liquidity, with large daily trading volumes.
- Extensive analyst coverage and media attention.
- Lower volatility compared to small-cap and micro-cap stocks.
- Strong corporate governance and operational transparency.

Why investors choose blue-chips: Blue-chip stocks are preferred for **stability, capital preservation, and steady returns**. They are less likely to deliver 10x or 50x gains quickly, but they provide a reliable foundation for long-term investment portfolios. They are ideal for investors prioritizing **safety and predictability** over explosive growth.

Comparing Risk and Reward Across Markets

Understanding the trade-offs between these categories is essential:

Category	**Market Cap**	**Volatility**	**Potential Returns**
Micro-Cap	¡$300M	Very High	Extremely High (10x+)
Small-Cap	$300M–$2B	High	High (5x–10x)
Blue-Chip	¿$10B	Low–Moderate	Moderate (1x–3x)

The general pattern is clear: **higher potential returns come with higher risk**. Micro-caps and small-caps, which include many penny stocks, can generate multibagger opportunities but require careful research, disciplined risk management, and patience. Blue-chips offer safety and stability but limited upside in comparison.

Why This Matters for Penny Stock Investors

For anyone pursuing penny stocks or multibagger potential, understanding where a stock sits in this spectrum is critical. Penny stocks typically fall into the **micro-cap or small-cap categories**, meaning they are inherently riskier but also capable of delivering extraordinary returns.

By comparing these categories:

- You can **align your investment strategy** with your risk tolerance and financial goals.
- You can identify the **types of companies** most likely to produce multi-bagger returns.
- You can apply **risk management techniques** appropriate for each market segment.

In summary, knowing the difference between micro-cap, small-cap, and blue-chip stocks is not just academic—it is foundational. It helps investors make informed decisions, balance risk and reward, and navigate the exciting yet volatile world of penny stock investing.

Key Takeaways

- **Penny stocks are legitimate, high-risk investments:** They are small-cap or micro-cap stocks with low prices, offering potential for extraordinary returns, but also carrying high volatility and liquidity risks.
- **Not all penny stocks are scams or illegal:** Myths about fraud, illegality, or unethical investing are exaggerated. Understanding regulation and ethical practices helps investors avoid pitfalls.
- **Global definitions vary but the principles remain consistent:** In the US, penny stocks are typically under $5; in India, under INR 10–20; globally, they are small, under-followed, and high-potential stocks.
- **History shapes behavior:** Penny stocks evolved from OTC markets to regulated exchanges like Nasdaq and NSE, increasing transparency, liquidity, and investor protection—but volatility and growth potential remain.
- **Micro-cap vs small-cap vs blue-chip:**
  - Micro-caps: Extremely high risk, extremely high potential returns (10x+).
  - Small-caps: High risk, high growth potential (5x–10x).
  - Blue-chips: Low risk, moderate returns (1x–3x).
- **Due diligence is essential:** Research company fundamentals, understand financials, track news, and verify regulatory compliance before investing.

- **Ethical and disciplined investing is possible:** Avoid herd mentality, hype, or unverified tips; focus on transparent companies and maintain a systematic approach.
- **Risk and reward are linked:** Penny stocks offer a path to multibagger returns, but only for disciplined, informed investors who manage their capital carefully.
- **Strategic mindset matters:** Understanding what penny stocks are, their history, myths, and market positioning is the foundation for building a repeatable multibagger investment strategy.

These takeaways summarize the essential concepts and provide a framework for approaching penny stocks with clarity, confidence, and a long-term, systematic perspective.

Chapter 2

Why Penny Stocks Exist

Penny stocks are more than just low-priced shares—they are the lifeblood of entrepreneurial growth and innovation. While mainstream investors often overlook these small-cap and micro-cap companies, penny stocks play a critical role in **funding early-stage businesses, supporting emerging sectors, and providing opportunities for outsized returns**.

At their core, penny stocks exist because traditional funding avenues are often inaccessible to small or nascent companies. Banks, venture capital, and institutional investors may hesitate to back businesses with limited track records, modest revenues, or high perceived risk. This creates a gap that penny stocks fill: **allowing companies to raise capital directly from retail and institutional investors** who are willing to embrace higher risk for potentially higher rewards.

Investors must also understand the **regulatory frameworks** that govern penny stocks. While these regulations exist to protect participants, they also introduce complexities such as reporting requirements, listing criteria, and the risk of delisting if companies fail to meet standards. These frameworks are essential for maintaining market integrity, but they also mean that penny stock investing requires vigilance, due diligence, and a disciplined approach.

Finally, the world of penny stocks is a delicate balance of **risk and reward**, historically producing both spectacular winners and dramatic failures. Examining case studies from global markets reveals how some small-cap companies have delivered multibagger returns—transforming modest investments into life-changing wealth—while others have faltered due to mismanagement, fraud, or market forces beyond their control. Understanding why penny stocks exist and the forces that shape their growth is the first step toward leveraging them intelligently in your investment journey.

In this chapter, we will explore the mechanisms behind penny stocks, why they are indispensable to entrepreneurship and innovation, and how informed investors can navigate this high-risk, high-reward landscape with confidence.

2.1 Fueling Entrepreneurial Growth

Penny stocks are more than just low-priced shares—they are a **catalyst for entrepreneurial growth** and innovation across global markets. These small-cap and micro-cap companies often face significant barriers in securing traditional funding from banks, venture capitalists, or institutional investors. Penny stocks provide a mechanism for these companies to **raise capital directly from investors**, enabling them to develop products, expand operations, and pursue ambitious growth strategies.

A Launchpad for Startups and Innovation

For many small businesses and emerging ventures, penny stocks serve as a **launchpad for innovation.** By issuing shares at low prices, companies can attract a broad base of investors, each contributing to the capital needed to fund research, product development, and market expansion.

Industries such as **renewable energy, biotechnology, fintech, and electric vehicles** often rely on small-scale funding to get off the ground. Several companies that started as micro-cap or penny stock entities later grew into mid-cap or even large-cap market leaders, illustrating how these tiny investments can lead to monumental growth over time.

Democratizing Access for Investors

Penny stocks do not just benefit companies—they also **democratize entrepreneurship for investors.** With relatively low entry points, retail investors can participate in the early stages of a company's growth. Unlike private equity or venture capital, which typically require high minimum investments, penny stocks allow anyone with modest capital to engage in wealth-building opportunities, **creating a symbiotic relationship between investors and entrepreneurs.**

This accessibility empowers investors to:

- Participate in early-stage company growth.
- Support innovative ventures that may otherwise lack funding.
- Experience potential multibagger returns if companies succeed.

Historical Case Studies of Growth Through Penny Stocks

Throughout history, penny stocks have enabled remarkable entrepreneurial journeys:

- **Technology Startups:** Several tech companies, initially trading at under $5 per share, raised capital to expand product offerings and capture new markets, eventually graduating to larger exchanges like Nasdaq or NSE.

- **Biotech Firms:** Small pharmaceutical companies have leveraged penny stock funding to finance expensive clinical trials and research, paving the way for groundbreaking treatments.
- **Emerging Market Enterprises:** In countries like India, Brazil, and China, micro-cap companies raised domestic and international funds through penny stock listings, driving local economic growth and creating employment.

Economic Significance of Penny Stocks

Beyond individual companies, penny stocks contribute significantly to **economic ecosystems**:

- **Encouraging innovation:** Funding provided via penny stocks enables experimentation and development of new technologies, products, and services.
- **Job creation:** Capital infusion allows companies to hire talent, expand teams, and grow operations, benefiting local and global economies.
- **Market efficiency:** Emerging companies challenge incumbents, stimulating competition and enhancing efficiency across sectors.

Balancing Risk and Reward

While penny stocks are powerful tools for entrepreneurial growth, they are inherently **high-risk** investments. Low liquidity, high volatility, and limited information can lead to significant losses if investors are unprepared. Therefore, understanding a company's fundamentals, management integrity, and growth potential is essential.

Key principles for investors:

- Conduct thorough research and due diligence.
- Avoid speculative hype or unverified market tips.
- Diversify investments to manage risk exposure.
- Align investments with long-term growth strategies.

Conclusion

Viewing penny stocks as a **vehicle for entrepreneurial growth** transforms the mindset from mere speculation to strategic participation in innovation. These small-cap and micro-cap companies fuel creativity, economic development, and wealth creation. For investors, approaching penny stocks with discipline, research, and ethical principles opens the door to participating in the success of tomorrow's market leaders, while also contributing positively to broader economic ecosystems.

2.2 Regulatory Frameworks and Delisting Risks

Investing in penny stocks can be exciting, but it is essential to understand the **regulatory environment** and the risks associated with delisting. Regulatory frameworks exist to protect investors, maintain market integrity, and ensure transparency, but they also introduce complexities that every penny stock investor must navigate.

The Role of Regulation in Penny Stock Markets

Regulatory bodies around the world oversee the operations of stock exchanges, brokerages, and listed companies. Their primary goals are:

- **Protecting investors:** Ensuring that companies provide accurate financial information and disclose material events.
- **Maintaining market integrity:** Preventing market manipulation, insider trading, and fraud.
- **Enhancing transparency:** Establishing rules for reporting, auditing, and governance.

In the United States, the **Securities and Exchange Commission (SEC)** regulates penny stocks under rules like the **Penny Stock Rule (SEC Rule 15g-9)**, which requires brokers to provide additional disclosures about risks, commissions, and market history before executing trades. Similarly, in India, the **Securities and Exchange Board of India (SEBI)** enforces strict listing requirements, continuous disclosures, and circuit filters to protect investors in low-priced and small-cap securities.

Globally, other markets such as Canada, the UK, and emerging economies have their own frameworks. While the rules differ, the **core principle is the same**: protect investors while allowing small companies to access public capital.

Delisting Risks: What Investors Must Know

One of the unique challenges of investing in penny stocks is the risk of **delisting**—the removal of a company's shares from an exchange. Delisting can occur voluntarily (e.g., mergers, acquisitions, or privatization) or involuntarily due to regulatory non-compliance or poor financial performance.

Common triggers for delisting include:

- Failure to meet minimum market capitalization or net worth thresholds.
- Inability to file audited financial statements on time.
- Persistent low share prices below exchange-specified limits.
- Non-compliance with corporate governance or disclosure regulations.

Delisting can have serious implications for investors: liquidity dries up, stock prices often collapse, and exit options become limited. While delisting does not always mean the company has failed, it does require **careful monitoring and risk management**.

Navigating the Regulatory Landscape

Understanding regulatory requirements is critical for protecting investments:

- **Know the exchange rules:** Each stock exchange has specific listing criteria, reporting requirements, and compliance standards.
- **Monitor disclosures:** Quarterly and annual financial statements, board announcements, and compliance filings are key indicators of company health.
- **Stay informed about regulatory changes:** Amendments to laws or rules can affect eligibility, trading restrictions, or investor protections.
- **Work with credible brokers:** Established platforms adhere to regulations and provide essential disclosures, minimizing exposure to illegal or unethical practices.

Balancing Opportunity and Compliance

While regulatory oversight might seem cumbersome, it is ultimately a **safeguard for investors**. Penny stocks inherently carry higher risk, but understanding the rules and monitoring compliance can significantly reduce the probability of catastrophic losses.

Successful investors balance **opportunity and compliance** by:

- Conducting thorough due diligence on both the company and its regulatory track record.
- Maintaining a diversified portfolio to mitigate delisting or compliance risks.
- Treating penny stock investing as a long-term, disciplined strategy rather than speculative gambling.

Conclusion

Regulatory frameworks and delisting rules are not obstacles—they are protective mechanisms that **allow investors to participate safely in high-risk, high-reward markets**. By understanding the rules, monitoring compliance, and staying disciplined, investors can leverage penny stocks as tools for wealth creation, while minimizing exposure to unnecessary risks.

Investing in penny stocks with awareness of regulatory and delisting risks is not just prudent—it is **essential for building a sustainable multibagger portfolio**.

2.3 Risk vs Reward with Historical Examples

Investing in penny stocks offers a **unique combination of extraordinary potential returns and significant risks**. Understanding this risk-reward spectrum is essential for any investor aiming to navigate the penny stock market successfully. While the allure of multibagger gains attracts traders, the reality of volatility, low liquidity, and business uncertainty cannot be ignored.

The Nature of Risk in Penny Stocks

Penny stocks are inherently risky for several reasons:

- **Volatility:** Prices can swing dramatically within hours, creating both opportunities and threats for investors.
- **Low liquidity:** Limited trading volume can make it difficult to enter or exit positions at desired prices.
- **Information asymmetry:** Small companies often have minimal public disclosures, leaving investors with incomplete data.
- **Manipulation risks:** Unscrupulous actors may engage in pump-and-dump schemes, artificially inflating stock prices before selling at a profit.

Despite these challenges, penny stocks are a **fertile ground for wealth creation** when approached with knowledge, discipline, and strategy.

The Reward Side: Multibagger Potential

The primary attraction of penny stocks is their **high-reward potential**. Historically, many small-cap or micro-cap companies have delivered returns of **10x, 20x, or even 50x**, transforming modest investments into life-changing wealth.

The low price per share means that even small investments can scale rapidly if the company experiences growth, innovation, or market recognition. This makes penny stocks particularly appealing for investors willing to take calculated risks and perform diligent research.

Historical Case Examples: Lessons Learned

Success Stories

- **Apple Inc. (1980s):** In its early days, Apple traded as a small-cap stock. Investors who recognized the company's innovative potential and held their positions saw exponential returns as the company grew into a global technology leader.

- **Monster Beverage (formerly Hansen's Natural):** Trading under $1 in the 1990s, Monster's stock multiplied over 1,000x for early investors after it captured the energy drink market.
- **Indian Penny Stocks:** Companies like Aegis Logistics and Info Edge started as micro-cap or low-priced stocks. Through consistent growth, strong fundamentals, and strategic market expansion, they delivered multibagger returns for disciplined early investors.

Cautionary Tales

- **Stratton Oakmont & Pump-and-Dump Stocks:** The infamous schemes of the 1980s and 1990s illustrate how hype and manipulation can temporarily inflate prices, only to leave unsuspecting investors with severe losses.
- **Failed Biotech Ventures:** Some penny stock biotech firms fail clinical trials or face regulatory hurdles, resulting in stock value collapse despite early investor optimism.
- **Micro-cap Pitfalls:** Companies with weak governance, high debt, or opaque operations may ultimately delist or go bankrupt, wiping out investor capital.

Balancing Risk and Reward Strategically

The lesson from history is clear: **risk and reward in penny stocks are inseparable**. Savvy investors employ strategies that maximize upside while mitigating downside:

- Conduct deep fundamental analysis to understand company viability.
- Use technical analysis to identify entry and exit points.
- Diversify across multiple penny stocks to reduce single-stock risk.
- Maintain disciplined position sizing to protect overall portfolio capital.
- Keep an informed perspective on market sentiment, news, and regulatory changes.

Key Insights for Investors

- **High risk can lead to high reward—but only with discipline.** Impulsive or uninformed trades increase the likelihood of losses.
- **Long-term perspective matters.** Many multibagger stocks require patience as companies scale, innovate, and gain market recognition.

- **Learn from both winners and losers.** Studying historical examples equips investors to identify patterns, avoid common mistakes, and replicate successful strategies.

Conclusion

Penny stocks are a **double-edged sword**: they offer the potential for life-changing gains while carrying inherent risks that can result in total capital loss. The most successful investors approach these markets with a **systematic, research-driven mindset**, combining knowledge of historical performance, fundamental and technical analysis, and disciplined risk management.

By embracing the lessons of the past and respecting the volatility of these small-cap markets, investors can tilt the risk-reward equation in their favor and increase the likelihood of uncovering the next multibagger opportunity.

Key Takeaways

- **Penny stocks drive entrepreneurial growth:** They provide crucial capital to startups and small businesses, enabling innovation, product development, and market expansion that might not be possible through traditional funding channels.
- **Democratization of investment:** Penny stocks allow retail investors with modest capital to participate in early-stage company growth, fostering a symbiotic relationship between investors and entrepreneurs.
- **Global relevance:** While rules and definitions vary across markets like India, the US, and other emerging economies, the fundamental purpose of penny stocks—to fund growth and enable investor participation—remains consistent.
- **Regulatory frameworks are protective, not restrictive:** Understanding the rules set by bodies like the SEC, SEBI, and other global regulators helps investors avoid fraud, manipulation, and compliance issues while navigating penny stock markets.
- **Delisting risks are real:** Companies may be delisted voluntarily or involuntarily due to poor performance, non-compliance, or mergers. Monitoring financial health and regulatory filings is essential to manage these risks.
- **High-risk, high-reward dynamic:** Penny stocks offer extraordinary potential gains, sometimes yielding 10x–50x returns, but they also carry significant volatility, low liquidity, and information gaps.
- **Learning from history is critical:** Case studies of both successful multibagger penny stocks and cautionary tales highlight the importance of research, due diligence, and disciplined investing.

- **Strategic approach is essential:** Investors should combine fundamental analysis, technical insights, diversification, and risk management to maximize upside while protecting capital.
- **Investor mindset matters:** Treat penny stocks as tools for systematic wealth creation rather than speculative gambling. Patience, research, and a long-term perspective significantly improve chances of success.

Final Thought: Penny stocks exist to fuel growth—for companies, for innovation, and for investors willing to engage with discipline and strategy. By understanding their role, risks, and opportunities, investors can participate in building the next generation of market leaders while creating potential for life-changing wealth.

Chapter 3

The Truth About Risk

Investing in penny stocks is not for the faint of heart. The market offers **tremendous upside potential**, but it is paired with unique risks that every investor must understand before committing capital. This chapter dives deep into the **truth about risk**, helping you differentiate between calculated opportunities and reckless speculation.

Penny stocks are often marketed as the gateway to **life-changing wealth**, and in many cases, they can be. With minimal capital, investors have the chance to discover multibagger opportunities—stocks that multiply several times over, creating extraordinary returns. The appeal is undeniable: for a small initial investment, the rewards can be exponential.

However, this potential comes with a **flip side**. Penny stocks are inherently volatile. Prices can swing dramatically within a single day, and liquidity is often limited, making it difficult to enter or exit positions at desired prices. Low regulatory oversight and opaque business practices in some markets can expose investors to scams, manipulation, and outright fraud.

Throughout this chapter, we will explore the **pros and cons** of penny stock investing, illustrated with **real-life examples of both spectacular wins and devastating losses**. By understanding these risks in context, you can cultivate a mindset that balances ambition with discipline, enabling you to participate in high-risk, high-reward opportunities **strategically and safely**.

In the sections that follow, you will learn to:

- Recognize the inherent advantages of penny stocks, including low capital requirements and multibagger potential.

- Identify the primary risks, from extreme volatility to market manipulation.

- Analyze real-world case studies to understand how successes and failures unfold in practice.

- Develop a risk-aware investment approach that maximizes opportunity while protecting capital.

This chapter will equip you with the **tools, knowledge, and perspective** needed to navigate the thrilling but unpredictable world of penny stocks, ensuring that every decision is informed, calculated, and aligned with your long-term wealth-building goals.

3.1 Pros: Low Capital, Multibagger Potential, High Upside

Penny stocks are often seen as the ultimate playground for small investors with big dreams. Unlike blue-chip stocks or large-cap companies, which may require substantial capital to achieve meaningful returns, penny stocks provide a **low-cost entry point** into the world of equity markets.

Low Capital Requirement: Accessibility for All

One of the most compelling advantages of penny stocks is that they **allow investors to start small**. Even with a modest budget, individuals can purchase a meaningful number of shares and participate in the growth story of a company. This democratization of investment makes penny stocks accessible to:

- Beginners who want to learn investing without risking large sums of money.
- Part-time traders with limited capital but strong market research skills.
- International investors seeking entry into emerging markets where stock prices are generally lower.

This low barrier to entry not only enables financial participation but also provides **practical experience in real-world markets**, helping investors develop skills in analysis, trading, and risk management.

Multibagger Potential: The Dream of Exponential Growth

Perhaps the most enticing aspect of penny stocks is their **multibagger potential**—the possibility that an investment can multiply several times over. Historical examples demonstrate that companies starting as micro-cap or penny stocks have gone on to deliver **10x, 20x, or even 50x returns** for early investors.

The reasons for this potential include:

- **Growth stage of the company:** Many penny stocks represent companies in the early phases of business development, where market penetration, product innovation, and operational scaling can drive rapid revenue and profit growth.
- **Undervalued market perception:** Because these companies are often under-followed by analysts and large institutional investors, there is untapped potential for price discovery when good news or strong performance emerges.
- **Emerging sectors:** Industries like renewable energy, electric vehicles, artificial intelligence, biotech, and fintech often have small-cap pioneers whose early investors reap outsized rewards when the sector expands.

Investors who can identify promising companies with strong fundamentals, a clear growth trajectory, and sound management have the opportunity to **turn modest investments into substantial wealth** over time.

High Upside Potential: Reward Proportional to Risk

The combination of low capital and multibagger potential leads naturally to **high upside potential**. A small investment in the right company can translate into significant gains, sometimes surpassing what large-cap stocks could achieve for the same initial capital.

Key factors contributing to this high upside include:

- **Price volatility:** While volatility introduces risk, it also creates opportunities for substantial short-term gains for informed and disciplined traders.
- **Market inefficiencies:** Penny stocks are often less followed, which means that positive developments—such as new contracts, product launches, or regulatory approvals—can lead to rapid price appreciation.
- **Leverage effect of compounding:** Reinvesting gains from successful penny stock investments can amplify returns over multiple cycles, turning small initial stakes into **life-changing wealth**.

Psychological Advantages: Engagement and Learning

Investing in penny stocks also has **intangible benefits**. Because the stakes are lower, investors can experiment, learn, and refine strategies without risking their entire capital. This hands-on experience accelerates learning in areas such as:

- Reading financial statements and balance sheets.
- Understanding market psychology and price movements.

- Applying technical analysis and chart patterns in real-time.
- Managing emotions such as fear, greed, and FOMO in highly volatile environments.

These skills not only improve penny stock investing success but also build a **foundation for broader investment competence**, applicable to mid-cap, large-cap, and even international markets.

Conclusion

The pros of penny stock investing—**low capital requirement, multibagger potential, and high upside**—make them a compelling choice for investors seeking exponential returns and hands-on learning. While these advantages come with inherent risks, a structured approach, disciplined analysis, and patient execution can allow investors to harness these benefits effectively.

When approached strategically, penny stocks offer a unique intersection of **accessibility, learning, and wealth-building potential**, creating opportunities that are rarely found in other areas of the stock market.

3.2 Cons: Volatility, Low Liquidity, Scams, Manipulation

While penny stocks offer exciting potential, it is crucial to **understand and respect the risks** involved. Unlike large-cap or well-established stocks, penny stocks operate in an environment characterized by high uncertainty and frequent market anomalies. Ignoring these risks can lead to significant financial losses, making risk management a critical skill for every investor.

Volatility: The Double-Edged Sword

Penny stocks are notoriously volatile. Prices can **swing dramatically within minutes or hours**, often without any clear fundamental reason. This extreme volatility arises from:

- **Low market capitalization:** Smaller companies have fewer shares outstanding, so even modest buy or sell orders can shift prices significantly.
- **Market sentiment sensitivity:** News, rumors, or social media buzz can trigger outsized price movements.
- **Speculative trading:** A high proportion of trades are often driven by short-term speculation rather than long-term fundamentals.

While volatility can create opportunities for rapid gains, it also exposes investors to **sudden and severe losses** if positions are not managed carefully.

Low Liquidity: Difficulty Entering and Exiting Positions

Liquidity refers to the ease with which an investor can buy or sell a stock without significantly affecting its price. Penny stocks often suffer from **low trading volumes**, which means:

- Large orders can move the stock price sharply against the investor.
- Selling shares quickly may require accepting a lower price, eroding potential gains.
- The market may be thin, with few buyers or sellers available at any given time, increasing execution risk.

Low liquidity magnifies risk and requires investors to plan carefully when entering and exiting positions, particularly for larger trades.

Scams: The Dark Side of Penny Stocks

The allure of rapid gains has historically attracted **fraudulent schemes** in the penny stock space. Common scams include:

- **Pump-and-dump schemes:** Scammers artificially inflate a stock's price through hype and misleading promotions, only to sell their holdings at a profit, leaving other investors with losses.
- **Insider manipulation:** Company insiders or promoters may trade shares to create a false perception of growth or demand.
- **Fraudulent filings and disclosures:** Inadequate or misleading reporting can mask poor performance, debt, or operational risks.

Being aware of these schemes and knowing how to identify red flags is essential to **protect your capital** and avoid falling victim to unethical practices.

Manipulation: Market Forces That Work Against Investors

Even legitimate penny stocks are vulnerable to **market manipulation** due to their small size and low visibility. Examples include:

- **Choppy trading patterns:** Price fluctuations caused by small orders or coordinated trades.

- **False news and social media hype:** Rumors or misleading posts on platforms like Reddit, Twitter, or Telegram can distort market sentiment.
- **Short-term speculative spikes:** Sharp, unsustainable price increases often precede rapid declines, catching unprepared investors off guard.

To navigate these risks, investors must combine **technical analysis, fundamental research, and disciplined exit strategies** to avoid being caught in manipulative cycles.

Risk Mitigation Strategies

Despite these challenges, risks in penny stocks can be **managed and mitigated** with the right approach:

- Diversify investments across multiple stocks to reduce exposure to a single company.
- Use position sizing and stop-loss orders to limit potential losses.
- Conduct thorough due diligence, analyzing financial statements, management quality, and market trends.
- Monitor news, announcements, and social sentiment critically, separating hype from reality.
- Approach penny stocks as **high-risk, high-reward components** of a broader portfolio rather than relying on them exclusively.

Conclusion

Penny stocks are exciting and potentially rewarding, but they exist in a **high-risk environment** defined by volatility, low liquidity, scams, and market manipulation. Success requires not just enthusiasm but **discipline, research, and a strategic mindset**. By understanding and respecting these risks, investors can participate safely in the penny stock market while maximizing the chances of uncovering genuine multibagger opportunities.

3.3 Real-Life Wins and Losses: Lessons from the Market

Investing in penny stocks is often portrayed as a fast track to wealth, but the reality is far more nuanced. The stories of real investors—both successes and failures—highlight **the fine line between strategic opportunity and reckless speculation**. Studying these cases provides invaluable insights into how to navigate this high-risk, high-reward market.

Case Study: The Spectacular Win

Consider a small-cap technology company in India that was trading under INR 10 per share in 2015. Early investors who conducted detailed research on its **financials, management, and sector potential** noticed its innovative product pipeline and strategic partnerships. Over the next five years, the company experienced exponential growth as its products gained market adoption, and its stock price skyrocketed to INR 500.

Key lessons from this success story include:

- **Patience pays off:** Long-term commitment and conviction in the company's fundamentals yielded extraordinary returns.
- **Thorough research is crucial:** Understanding the business model, market size, and competitive advantages allowed investors to separate true potential from hype.
- **Diversification still matters:** Those who allocated only a portion of their portfolio to this stock enjoyed wealth creation without risking all their capital.

Case Study: The Devastating Loss

In contrast, another investor purchased shares of a micro-cap company heavily promoted on social media and through newsletters. The stock, trading at $0.50, doubled in a few days due to hype rather than fundamentals. The investor increased exposure, ignoring warning signs, only to see the price collapse when the promotion ended and insiders sold their shares. The investment was almost completely wiped out within weeks.

Key lessons from this failure include:

- **Beware of hype and pump-and-dump schemes:** Quick price spikes driven by rumors or promotion rarely reflect genuine value.
- **Discipline is essential:** Emotional trading and chasing gains often lead to catastrophic losses.
- **Due diligence cannot be skipped:** Understanding the company's financial health and regulatory compliance can prevent exposure to manipulated stocks.

Patterns Across Wins and Losses

By comparing multiple case studies globally—from Nasdaq penny stocks to Indian small-cap gems—a few consistent patterns emerge:

- **Research wins, speculation loses:** Long-term winners are identified through careful analysis, not guesswork.

- **Volatility is both friend and foe:** Smart investors leverage volatility for entry and exit points, while reckless traders suffer losses from sudden swings.
- **Timing and patience matter:** Many multibaggers require years of holding, while impulsive trades chasing short-term spikes often fail.
- **Risk management is non-negotiable:** Successful investors use stop-losses, position sizing, and portfolio diversification to minimize catastrophic losses.

The Psychological Lesson

Beyond numbers, these stories teach a psychological lesson: **control over emotion and rational decision-making is as important as market knowledge**. Fear, greed, and impatience can erode even the most promising investment. Conversely, disciplined thinking and a long-term perspective amplify the odds of turning small investments into multibagger outcomes.

Conclusion

Real-life wins and losses in penny stocks highlight that extraordinary returns are possible—but never guaranteed. Every success story is matched by cautionary tales, emphasizing that **knowledge, discipline, and strategic action** determine outcomes more than luck. By learning from these examples, investors can develop a mindset and methodology that maximizes potential gains while minimizing unnecessary risk.

Key Takeaways

- **Low Capital Requirement:** Penny stocks allow investors to enter the market with modest amounts of money, making them accessible to beginners and small-scale traders.
- **Multibagger Potential:** With careful research and strategic investing, small investments in penny stocks can grow exponentially, delivering 10x, 20x, or even 50x returns in favorable scenarios.
- **High Upside Rewards:** The combination of low capital and growth potential means investors can achieve life-changing wealth if they identify and hold the right opportunities over time.
- **High Volatility:** Prices of penny stocks can fluctuate sharply in short periods due to low market capitalization, speculative trading, and sensitivity to news and rumors.
- **Low Liquidity:** Limited trading volume can make it difficult to enter or exit positions without affecting prices, increasing execution risk.

- **Susceptibility to Scams:** Penny stocks are often targeted by pump-and-dump schemes, insider manipulation, and fraudulent practices, requiring vigilance and due diligence.
- **Market Manipulation Risks:** Small-cap companies are more easily influenced by social media hype, false news, or coordinated trading, which can create misleading price movements.
- **Real-Life Lessons Matter:** Studying actual wins and losses teaches investors the importance of research, discipline, patience, and emotional control. Success comes from a strategic approach, not luck.
- **Risk Management is Essential:** Using stop-losses, diversification, careful position sizing, and disciplined exit strategies helps mitigate losses while still participating in high-upside opportunities.
- **Mindset and Strategy Trump Luck:** Investors who combine analytical rigor with emotional discipline increase their chances of achieving sustainable, long-term wealth in penny stocks.

Final Thought: Penny stocks embody a high-risk, high-reward environment. Understanding both the opportunities and the dangers, learning from real-world cases, and applying disciplined risk management are essential for converting small investments into meaningful, multibagger wealth.

Chapter 4

Penny Stocks vs Other Investments

Investing is not a one-size-fits-all endeavor. Different asset classes offer varying levels of risk, liquidity, and return potential. In this chapter, we compare penny stocks with other popular investment options, including **blue-chip stocks, mid- and small-cap equities, cryptocurrencies, and options trading**, to help you understand where penny stocks fit into a diversified strategy.

While blue-chip stocks are often seen as the safest option, offering steady dividends and slow, predictable growth, they rarely deliver the kind of explosive returns that small-cap or penny stocks can provide. Similarly, cryptocurrencies and options offer high-risk, high-reward opportunities, but they require specialized knowledge and can be extremely volatile, sometimes decoupled from underlying fundamentals.

Penny stocks occupy a unique space in the investment landscape. Because they represent **smaller, often undervalued companies**, they provide a fertile ground for multibagger returns—investments that can multiply several times over. Understanding why these returns are concentrated in smaller companies, rather than large-cap blue chips, is critical for investors seeking extraordinary growth while managing risk.

Throughout this chapter, we will explore **historical multibagger case studies**, highlighting how certain small-cap and penny stocks have transformed modest investments into substantial wealth. By the end, you will gain a clear perspective on how penny stocks compare to other investment vehicles and how they can strategically fit into your portfolio for long-term wealth creation.

4.1 Comparing Penny Stocks with Other Investment Options

To understand the true potential and role of penny stocks in a portfolio, it's essential to **compare them with other popular investment vehicles**. Each asset class—whether blue-chip stocks, small-cap equities, cryptocurrencies, or options—offers distinct advantages and limitations. This comparison will help investors appreciate why penny stocks can deliver outsized returns, while also highlighting the risks involved.

Blue-Chip Stocks: Stability Over Explosive Growth

Blue-chip stocks represent well-established companies with **large market capitalizations, consistent earnings, and proven track records**. Examples include companies like Apple, Microsoft, or Reliance Industries.

Key characteristics:

- **Lower Risk:** Blue-chips are generally less volatile and provide a sense of security for long-term investors.
- **Predictable Dividends:** Regular dividend payouts make them attractive for income-focused investors.
- **Slower Growth:** While stable, blue-chips rarely offer the exponential gains seen in small-cap or penny stocks.

For investors seeking **wealth preservation and modest, consistent returns**, blue-chip stocks are ideal. However, for those aiming for multibagger potential, the slow growth trajectory of blue-chips limits upside.

Small-Cap Stocks: The Sweet Spot Between Growth and Risk

Small-cap stocks typically represent companies with **market capitalizations between 300*millionand*2 billion**, bridging the gap between penny stocks and large-cap equities.

Advantages:

- **Higher Growth Potential:** Small-caps are often in expansion phases, capable of significant revenue and stock price growth.
- **Institutional Interest:** They attract attention from analysts and institutional investors, providing better market oversight than penny stocks.
- **Diversification Potential:** Small-caps can complement blue-chip holdings in a diversified portfolio.

However, they still carry **higher volatility** than blue-chips, making them riskier than established companies but less speculative than penny stocks.

Cryptocurrencies: High-Risk, Speculative Assets

Cryptocurrencies, such as Bitcoin, Ethereum, and emerging altcoins, have surged in popularity as **alternative investment vehicles.**

Key points of comparison:

- **Extreme Volatility:** Crypto prices can swing 20–50% in a single day, often decoupled from underlying fundamentals.
- **Speculative Nature:** Unlike stocks, cryptos do not represent ownership in a company or underlying business value.
- **High Reward Potential:** Despite risk, early investors in coins like Bitcoin or Ethereum have realized extraordinary returns, similar to multibagger penny stocks.

While cryptocurrencies can offer high upside, their speculative nature, lack of intrinsic cash flows, and regulatory uncertainties differentiate them from penny stocks, which at least have **a tangible underlying business.**

Options Trading: Leveraged Risk and Strategy

Options are derivatives that give the right, but not the obligation, to buy or sell an asset at a predetermined price within a specified period.

Advantages:

- **Leverage:** Small capital can control large positions, magnifying potential returns.
- **Flexibility:** Options can be used for hedging, income generation, or speculative strategies.

Drawbacks:

- **Complexity:** Options require understanding of strategies, Greeks, and time decay.
- **High Risk of Total Loss:** Incorrect positioning can lead to the complete loss of invested capital.

Compared to penny stocks, options offer **controlled risk exposure through defined contracts**, but they are less accessible for beginners and lack the long-term compounding potential of equity investments.

Why Penny Stocks Stand Out

When compared to these alternatives:

- **Potential for Multibagger Returns:** Unlike blue-chips or small-caps, certain penny stocks can multiply many times over if the underlying company succeeds.
- **Low Initial Investment:** Entry costs are minimal compared to options or large-cap stocks.
- **Direct Ownership of a Business:** Unlike crypto, penny stocks represent shares in an actual operating company with tangible revenue and assets.

However, the trade-off is **higher risk**. Investors must accept volatility, lower liquidity, and susceptibility to manipulation as part of the penny stock experience. With research, discipline, and strategy, penny stocks occupy a unique position in a portfolio, offering opportunities that other investment vehicles often cannot match.

Conclusion

Understanding the characteristics of blue-chip stocks, small-cap equities, cryptocurrencies, and options allows investors to contextualize penny stocks within the broader investment landscape. While each asset class serves a purpose, penny stocks are particularly **suited for investors seeking high-risk, high-reward growth opportunities** with the potential for life-changing returns.

4.2 Why Multibagger Returns Are Concentrated in Small-Cap and Penny Stocks

Multibagger returns—investments that multiply several times over—are the holy grail of wealth creation in the stock market. While large-cap and blue-chip stocks provide steady, predictable growth, the **biggest wealth-generating opportunities often reside in small-cap and penny stocks.** Understanding why requires exploring market dynamics, company growth potential, and investor behavior.

Small Size, Big Opportunity

Penny and small-cap stocks are typically **companies with lower market capitalization**, often under $300 million globally or equivalent in local currencies. Their small size creates fertile ground for exponential growth:

- **Underfollowed by Analysts:** Unlike large-cap stocks, these companies receive limited coverage from analysts and institutional investors, creating inefficiencies in pricing.

- **Undervalued Potential:** Many of these businesses are early in their growth journey, meaning their stock prices may not yet reflect future revenues, market share, or profit potential.
- **Scalable Business Models:** Small companies often operate in emerging sectors or niches, where successful products or services can dramatically increase valuation in a relatively short time.

Because of these factors, **a relatively small improvement in operations, product adoption, or market perception can result in massive stock price appreciation**—the essence of a multibagger.

Higher Risk, Higher Reward

Multibagger opportunities are concentrated in penny and small-cap stocks largely because **risk and return are correlated**. Larger, well-established companies have lower risk profiles, but their size and market penetration limit explosive growth:

- A blue-chip company doubling its revenue is far more difficult than a small-cap startup achieving the same relative growth.
- Volatility in small-cap and penny stocks, while risky, enables the **potential for dramatic upward movements** in stock prices.
- Investors willing to take calculated risks and conduct rigorous due diligence are positioned to capture these outsized gains.

Market Inefficiencies and Discovery Potential

Small-cap and penny stocks are often **undervalued or mispriced** due to:

- Limited analyst coverage and media attention.
- Infrequent trading and low liquidity, making it harder for prices to immediately reflect new developments.
- Lack of institutional ownership, leaving room for **retail investors to identify overlooked gems**.

These inefficiencies create opportunities for observant, disciplined investors to find stocks that have the potential to grow several-fold before the broader market catches on.

Historical Examples of Multibagger Success

Across markets worldwide, small-cap and penny stocks have produced extraordinary returns:

- **India:** Several small-cap technology and pharma companies went from INR 5–10 per share to INR 500+ within a decade, driven by product adoption, regulatory approvals, and strong management execution.
- **United States:** Early investors in companies like Apple or Amazon, which started as relatively small-cap stocks, saw returns that exceeded 100x over multiple decades.
- **Emerging Markets:** In countries with rapidly developing sectors, undervalued small-cap stocks in fintech, renewable energy, and consumer products have delivered multibagger outcomes.

These examples demonstrate that **significant wealth is rarely generated in established, slow-growing companies**—it is often the smaller, high-growth enterprises that multiply investor capital dramatically.

Key Factors Driving Multibagger Returns

Several core elements make small-cap and penny stocks fertile ground for multibagger gains:

- **Innovative Products or Services:** Unique offerings in growing markets attract attention and revenue.
- **Operational Efficiency:** Companies that scale operations effectively can increase profit margins and stock value rapidly.
- **Sector Tailwinds:** Emerging industries (e.g., AI, EVs, renewable energy) provide an external growth engine.
- **Management Execution:** Strong leadership, vision, and disciplined capital allocation amplify growth potential.
- **Investor Awareness and Timing:** Early identification and patient holding of underpriced stocks allow investors to capture the full upside.

The Takeaway

Multibagger returns are concentrated in penny and small-cap stocks because **they combine growth potential, market inefficiencies, and investor-accessible opportunities**. While the risks are higher, the rewards for disciplined, informed, and patient investors can be transformative. Understanding this dynamic is essential for anyone seeking to move beyond average returns and explore the wealth-building potential of small-cap markets.

Final Thought: To identify potential multibaggers, investors must look beyond headline stocks, dig into fundamentals, monitor market trends, and maintain a **long-term perspective**. Small-cap and penny stocks are where careful research, strategic vision, and patience intersect to create extraordinary wealth.

4.3 Historical Multibagger Case Studies

Understanding the theory behind multibagger returns is important, but **real-world examples bring these concepts to life**. Across global markets, certain small-cap and penny stocks have delivered extraordinary returns to investors who identified opportunities early and exercised patience, discipline, and research. This section explores historical case studies that illustrate the power and risk of multibagger investing.

India: Small-Cap Success Stories

India has been a fertile ground for multibagger small-cap stocks, especially in sectors like technology, pharmaceuticals, and consumer goods.

- **Company A (Tech Sector)**: Listed at INR 5 per share, this small software firm leveraged India's IT boom in the 2000s. Over a decade, consistent product innovation, global contracts, and operational efficiency helped the stock reach INR 250—a 50x return for early investors. Lessons include identifying **emerging sector trends** and **evaluating management execution**.
- **Company B (Pharma Sector)**: Starting as a micro-cap at INR 10, this pharmaceutical company invested heavily in R&D, launched critical niche products, and captured domestic and international markets. Within 7 years, the stock surged to INR 600, illustrating the impact of **innovative products and regulatory approvals**.
- **Company C (Consumer Goods)**: Initially overlooked, this firm scaled rapidly in rural and semi-urban markets, riding the wave of consumer demand and branding initiatives. Early investors enjoyed more than 30x returns in under a decade. The key takeaway: even **consumer-oriented businesses with low capital bases** can become multibaggers with the right strategy.

United States: From Small Caps to Global Giants

Even in mature markets like the U.S., companies that began as small-cap or underfollowed stocks created massive wealth:

- **Apple Inc.**: While now a blue-chip giant, Apple was a relatively small-cap company in the early 1980s. Early investors who held the stock through multiple product cycles and market corrections saw returns exceeding 10,000% over several decades. Key lesson: **innovative products + long-term holding = transformative wealth**.

- **Amazon.com**: Starting as a small online bookseller, Amazon's stock was modestly priced during its IPO in 1997. Over the next two decades, as it expanded into e-commerce, cloud computing, and logistics, early investors experienced staggering returns. The lesson emphasizes **spotting scalable business models in growth industries**.
- **Tesla Inc.**: Tesla's early stock, considered highly risky and speculative, rewarded investors who believed in EV adoption and held through volatility. This shows that **high conviction, research, and patience can turn risky opportunities into multibagger outcomes**.

Emerging Markets: High-Risk, High-Reward

Emerging markets often harbor overlooked small-cap stocks with explosive growth potential due to untapped consumer markets, favorable policies, or infrastructure development.

- **Brazilian Renewable Energy Company**: An early entrant in solar and wind power, the company leveraged government incentives and rising energy demand. Its stock multiplied more than 20x within 5 years, demonstrating how **policy tailwinds and first-mover advantage** can create multibaggers.
- **Southeast Asian Fintech Startup**: Initially a micro-cap, this fintech firm tapped into underserved banking populations, scaling operations across multiple countries. Within 6 years, the stock increased more than 15-fold. The lesson: **market penetration in high-growth sectors drives extraordinary returns**.

Common Patterns Across Multibaggers

Analyzing these historical examples reveals recurring themes:

- **Early Identification**: Investors who recognize emerging trends, technologies, or sectors early enjoy disproportionate rewards.
- **Strong Management Teams**: Leadership that can scale operations, execute strategy, and navigate risks is a common thread in multibagger stories.
- **Long-Term Commitment**: Holding through volatility and avoiding impulsive decisions is crucial. Multibagger returns rarely happen overnight.

- **Sector Tailwinds**: Companies operating in growing or transformative industries tend to outperform.
- **Fundamental Strength**: Sustainable earnings, manageable debt, and scalable business models separate winners from those that fail.

Takeaways for Investors

Historical multibagger case studies highlight that **wealth creation is possible with small, undervalued, or overlooked stocks**, but it requires:

- Rigorous research and fundamental analysis.
- Patience and emotional discipline during market swings.
- Awareness of sector trends and macroeconomic factors.
- Strategic diversification to manage risk while participating in high-upside opportunities.

Final Thought: History teaches that multibagger returns are not random luck—they result from **early recognition, informed decision-making, and disciplined execution.** Penny stocks and small-caps offer a unique avenue to access these opportunities, provided investors approach them with preparation, patience, and strategy.

Key Takeaways

- **Early Identification is Critical:** Spotting emerging trends, technologies, or sectors before they gain mainstream attention is the first step toward multibagger returns.
- **Strong Management Drives Growth:** Companies with visionary, disciplined, and execution-focused leadership are more likely to scale successfully and deliver outsized returns.
- **Patience Pays Off:** Multibagger outcomes typically unfold over years. Holding through market volatility and avoiding impulsive reactions is essential.
- **Sector Tailwinds Amplify Returns:** Operating in high-growth or transformative industries—such as technology, renewable energy, fintech, or pharmaceuticals—can significantly increase upside potential.
- **Fundamentals Matter:** Sustainable earnings, low debt, strong cash flow, and scalable business models separate long-term winners from fleeting opportunities.

- **Global Opportunities Exist:** Multibagger potential is not limited to one market. Investors can find opportunities across India, the U.S., and emerging economies by understanding local market dynamics.
- **Diversification Mitigates Risk:** While small-cap and penny stocks carry high upside, a balanced approach across sectors, market caps, and geographies helps manage overall portfolio risk.
- **Learning from History:** Studying past multibagger examples provides actionable insights into patterns of growth, risk management, and the timing needed to maximize returns.

Final Thought: Multibagger investing is a blend of research, discipline, timing, and patience. While history does not guarantee future returns, understanding the principles and patterns behind past successes gives investors a structured framework to pursue high-growth opportunities strategically.

Part II

Getting Started

Chapter 5

Choosing Platforms & Accounts

Selecting the right trading platform is one of the most critical steps for any investor, especially when dealing with penny stocks and small-cap opportunities. The platform you choose affects **your market access, execution speed, analytical tools, fees, and overall trading experience**. A well-chosen platform can empower you to spot opportunities early, manage risk effectively, and execute trades efficiently, while the wrong choice can lead to missed opportunities, higher costs, or confusion.

5.1 Selecting the Right Trading Platform

Choosing the right trading platform is one of the most important decisions you will make as an investor, particularly when dealing with penny stocks and small-cap opportunities. The platform you select is more than just a tool to execute trades—it is the environment in which you will research, analyze, and act on investment opportunities. A poorly chosen platform can slow your decisions, increase your costs, and limit access to critical market data, while the right platform empowers you to trade confidently and efficiently.

Why Platform Choice Matters

Every platform differs in terms of **market access, fees, tools, usability, and regulatory protection**. Your choice will influence:

- How easily you can access penny stocks across different exchanges.
- The quality of research, charts, and technical indicators available.
- Speed and reliability of order execution.

- Costs, including commissions, spreads, and hidden fees.
- Convenience of use, whether you prefer mobile trading or desktop applications.

Selecting a platform is not about picking the "most popular" or "flashiest" option; it is about **matching the platform to your trading style, experience level, and investment goals**.

Global Perspective

Investors operate in different markets, and each region has its own set of dominant platforms:

- **India:** Platforms like Groww, Zerodha, and Angel One are widely used for NSE and BSE stocks, including penny and small-cap stocks. They vary in simplicity, research tools, and fees.
- **United States:** Robinhood, Webull, and Fidelity dominate the NASDAQ and NYSE space. They differ in interface design, analytical capabilities, and account types. Some prioritize ease of use, while others provide professional-grade tools.
- **Europe and UK:** Trading 212 and other regulated brokers offer access to European exchanges. Consider regulatory oversight, fractional investing options, and cross-border fees when selecting a platform.

Key Considerations

When evaluating a platform, ask yourself:

1. **Market Access:** Can it give you the exchanges and stock types you want?
2. **Tools and Features:** Are charts, screeners, and alerts sufficient for your strategy?
3. **Cost Efficiency:** How much will trading, withdrawals, and currency conversions cost?
4. **User Experience:** Does the interface suit your level of expertise? Is it easy to navigate and reliable?
5. **Device Flexibility:** Does it work well on mobile, desktop, or both?
6. **Safety and Regulation:** Is the platform regulated, and does it protect your funds?

Final Thoughts

The right platform becomes your trading backbone. It should not dictate your strategy but support it. By carefully evaluating market access, fees, tools, usability, and regulatory protections, you can select a platform that allows you to **execute trades efficiently, analyze opportunities effectively, and grow your investments safely over time**. Remember, a well-chosen platform is not just a convenience—it is a strategic advantage in your penny stock journey.

5.2 Step-by-Step Account Creation and Enabling Penny Stock Trading

Before you can start trading penny stocks, you must first set up a trading account with a brokerage. While specific steps vary by platform and country, the process generally follows a structured pattern. This section provides a **comprehensive, step-by-step guide** applicable to most global platforms, ensuring you can begin trading safely and efficiently.

1. Choose Your Brokerage Platform

Begin by selecting a platform that matches your region, trading goals, and experience level. Consider factors such as market access, fees, research tools, device usability, and regulatory protection. Refer to the previous section on "Selecting the Right Trading Platform" for guidance.

2. Register Your Account

1. Visit the official website or download the mobile app of your chosen platform.
2. Click on "Sign Up" or "Open Account."
3. Provide personal details: full name, email address, phone number, and country of residence.
4. Set up a secure password and, if available, enable two-factor authentication for additional security.

3. Complete Identity Verification

Regulated platforms require identity verification to comply with Know Your Customer (KYC) regulations. This step ensures your account is legitimate and protected:

- Upload government-issued ID (passport, driver's license, or national ID).

- Provide proof of address (utility bill, bank statement, or rental agreement).
- Some platforms may request additional verification, such as a selfie or video call.

4. Link Your Bank Account or Payment Method

To fund your trading account and withdraw profits, link a bank account or other approved payment method. Ensure the account is in your name and supports local currency transactions to minimize conversion fees.

5. Fund Your Account

Deposit an initial amount suitable for your trading plan. Start small, especially if you are testing penny stock strategies. Most platforms allow minimum deposits as low as \$10–\$50 (or equivalent local currency). Always confirm deposit limits and processing times.

6. Enable Penny Stock Trading

Not all platforms automatically allow trading in low-priced or small-cap stocks. To enable penny stock trading:

- Check the platform's terms for trading low-priced equities.
- Some brokers may require you to apply for additional permissions or enable advanced trading features.
- Familiarize yourself with risk disclosures, as penny stocks are highly volatile and may carry higher regulatory requirements.

7. Familiarize Yourself with Platform Tools

Before placing real trades, explore the platform's features:

- Learn how to search for penny stocks and add them to a watchlist.
- Understand charting tools, technical indicators, and news feeds.
- Test order types (market, limit, stop-loss) using small trades or paper trading if available.

8. Start Small and Monitor Performance

Begin trading with a small portion of your capital to test your strategy and the platform's functionality. Track each trade, analyze results, and adjust your approach before scaling up.

Global Considerations

- U.S. investors must ensure compliance with FINRA and SEC regulations, including penny stock rules under Rule 15c2-11.
- European investors should verify platform regulation by ESMA or local authorities.
- Indian investors must adhere to SEBI guidelines and trading limits for small-cap and low-priced stocks.

Conclusion

By carefully following these steps, you ensure that your trading account is **secure, compliant, and ready for penny stock trading**. This structured approach reduces risk, avoids common setup errors, and prepares you for a disciplined, informed investment journey.

5.3 Beginner vs Advanced Tools; Mobile vs Desktop; Fees Comparison

Once your trading account is set up and ready for penny stock trading, the next step is understanding the tools, platforms, and cost structures available to you. This knowledge is essential for **executing trades efficiently, analyzing stocks effectively, and optimizing returns**. Choosing the right combination of tools and interfaces depends on your experience, trading style, and the markets you operate in.

Beginner vs Advanced Tools

Trading platforms offer a spectrum of tools, from simple interfaces for beginners to advanced analytical systems for professional traders:

- **Beginner Tools:** These are designed for new investors and focus on simplicity and accessibility. Features often include:
  - Easy-to-read dashboards and watchlists.
  - Quick search for stocks by name or ticker.
  - Basic charts and pre-configured technical indicators.
  - Educational resources, tutorials, and alerts.

  Beginner-friendly tools reduce the cognitive load and allow investors to focus on learning fundamentals, identifying opportunities, and building confidence without being overwhelmed.

- **Advanced Tools:** Professional-grade platforms provide a comprehensive toolkit for technical analysis, strategy testing, and high-frequency trading. Features include:
  - Customizable charting with multiple timeframes, overlays, and indicators.
  - Screener tools to filter stocks based on technical and fundamental criteria.
  - Paper trading and simulation environments to test strategies.
  - Integration with APIs, automated alerts, and advanced order types (stop-limit, bracket orders, trailing stops).

  Advanced tools empower experienced traders to make data-driven decisions, identify micro-trends, and optimize entry and exit points.

Mobile vs Desktop Platforms

The choice between mobile and desktop interfaces is critical and often depends on your trading style:

- **Mobile Platforms:** Convenient for investors who trade on the go, mobile apps offer real-time quotes, watchlists, basic charts, and trade execution. While modern mobile platforms are powerful, some advanced features like deep analytics and multi-screen layouts are limited.
- **Desktop Platforms:** Desktop applications provide a larger workspace for charting, technical analysis, and multitasking. They often include more comprehensive tools, faster execution, and the ability to monitor multiple markets simultaneously. For serious traders or those executing intraday strategies, desktops are typically preferred.

Many modern brokers provide **synchronized experiences**, allowing you to start analysis on desktop and execute trades on mobile, combining the best of both worlds.

Fees and Cost Considerations

Costs vary widely across platforms and can significantly impact returns, particularly in penny stock trading:

- **Commissions:** Some platforms charge per trade, while others offer commission-free trading. Always check if restrictions apply to low-priced or small-cap stocks.
- **Spreads:** The difference between buy and sell prices can add to trading costs, especially for low-liquidity penny stocks.

- **Account Maintenance Fees:** Some brokers charge annual or monthly fees, particularly for premium tools or margin accounts.
- **Currency Conversion:** For cross-border trading, conversion fees can add up if your account and stock are in different currencies.

Understanding fees ensures that you **maximize profits, avoid unnecessary costs, and select the platform that aligns with your trading frequency and capital.**

Choosing the Right Combination

- Beginners may prefer **mobile-first platforms with simple dashboards, low or no fees, and basic charts**. - Intermediate traders often benefit from **desktop platforms with additional indicators, screeners, and moderate fees**. - Advanced traders require **full-featured desktop platforms with customizable tools, API integration, automated alerts, and competitive fee structures**.

The key is to match your platform, tools, and interface to your **experience level, trading style, and investment goals**, ensuring that your focus remains on identifying opportunities and managing risk, rather than struggling with the technology itself.

Key Takeaways

- **Your trading platform is your cockpit.** The right platform doesn't just execute trades it shapes how you analyze opportunities, manage risk, and respond to market movements. Choose one that aligns with your comfort level, trading style, and long-term goals rather than chasing trends or flashy interfaces.
- **Understand regional accessibility.** Platforms vary globally. Indian investors might favor Groww, Zerodha, or Angel One for local exchanges, while international traders may lean toward Robinhood, Webull, Fidelity, or Trading 212. What matters most is not the brand, but reliability, transparency, and execution speed.
- **Account setup is foundational, not complicated.** Modern brokers have simplified onboarding. With a few verification steps ID, bank link, and KYC you can open a trading account within hours. However, ensure you enable penny stock trading permissions, as many platforms restrict OTC or micro-cap trades by default.
- **Match tools to your experience level.** Beginners benefit from clean, mobile-first interfaces with educational support and simple dashboards. Advanced traders thrive on platforms offering screeners, technical indicators, API access, and advanced order types. The best system is the one that you can use confidently and consistently.

- **Mobile vs desktop is about lifestyle, not hierarchy.** Mobile apps offer accessibility and convenience for monitoring markets, while desktop platforms provide depth, multi-screen analysis, and precision for active traders. Many successful investors use both analysis on desktop, execution on mobile.

- **Fees quietly shape your returns.** Always factor in commissions, spreads, maintenance costs, and conversion charges. In penny stock trading, even small differences in fees can erode profits because margins are often thin. Choose cost-efficient brokers without compromising on execution speed or support.

- **Platform reliability outweighs popularity.** A flashy app means nothing if it crashes during high volatility. Prioritize stability, regulatory compliance, and customer service over marketing hype. Your platform should empower you not stress you.

- **Evolve your setup as you grow.** Start simple. As your skill, capital, and confidence increase, upgrade your tools, analytics, and trading environment. Every professional once began with a basic account what matters is how you build mastery over time.

In essence, choosing your platform and account is not about finding the "best" broker it's about finding the one that best fits *you*. The right platform acts as an extension of your trading philosophy: secure, efficient, and aligned with your goals. Get this foundation right, and every decision thereafter becomes sharper and more confident.

Chapter 6

How to Buy, Sell, and Trade Like a Pro

Trading is not just about clicking a "Buy" or "Sell" button it's about executing a well-researched plan with discipline, timing, and emotional control. In penny stocks, where fortunes can shift within minutes, the difference between an amateur and a professional isn't access to information it's how they interpret, act, and manage risk.

This chapter transforms theory into practice. You'll learn how to enter and exit trades strategically, recognize market setups, and develop instincts that come only from structured experience. We'll move step-by-step through buying and selling processes from placing your first order to using advanced trade types like limit and stop-loss.

Whether you're trading intraday, swing, or long-term, the core principles remain the same: protect your capital, follow a repeatable system, and let probability not emotion guide your decisions.

You'll also explore **paper trading** a risk-free method of practicing real trades in simulated environments. Before risking a single rupee or dollar, you'll learn to build muscle memory through mock portfolios and trading simulators, sharpening your skills without financial stress.

By the end of this chapter, you'll understand:

- How to confidently execute buy and sell orders across platforms.
- The key differences between intraday, swing, and long-term strategies.
- How to use stop-losses, position sizing, and trade journaling like a professional.
- How to practice trading safely with paper trading tools before going live.

The goal isn't to turn you into a gambler chasing spikes it's to help you become a disciplined trader who plays the long game. This is where penny stock speculation turns into strategy where chaos becomes control, and potential becomes performance.

6.1 Step-by-Step Buying and Selling Strategies

Buying and selling penny stocks may seem as simple as pressing a button but in reality, it's a skill built on structure, timing, and patience. Every trade you make represents a small decision in your larger financial journey. The professionals don't rely on luck or hype; they rely on systems, probabilities, and consistency. This section walks you through that system the practical process of executing trades like a seasoned investor.

1. Preparing Before You Trade

Every successful trade begins long before you enter the market. Preparation is the most underrated step in trading, yet it separates consistent winners from emotional gamblers.

Before you even log in to your trading platform:

- Review your watchlist and identify 2–3 potential stocks that meet your screening criteria strong fundamentals, clear catalysts, or technical breakouts.
- Read the latest company news, earnings, or announcements that could influence movement.
- Define your exact **entry price, stop-loss, and target levels.** These are your guardrails once set, they protect you from impulsive decisions.

Professional traders often say, *"Amateurs enter trades. Professionals enter plans."* Treat every trade as a plan that you execute not a reaction to market excitement.

2. Understanding Order Types

Every market order is a signal it tells the system how you want to participate. Choosing the right order type determines whether you enter efficiently or end up paying more than you intended.

Common Order Types:

- **Market Order:** Executes immediately at the current price. Best for highly liquid stocks, but risky for volatile penny stocks since prices can change within seconds.
- **Limit Order:** Executes only at your chosen price or better. This is the preferred method for penny stocks it keeps you in control of entry cost.

- **Stop-Loss Order:** Automatically sells your position if the price falls below a defined threshold, preventing deep losses.
- **Stop-Limit Order:** Combines protection with precision it triggers a limit sell once the stop price is hit, ensuring you don't sell too low during sudden volatility.

In fast-moving markets, these tools are your armor. Professionals never enter a trade without knowing exactly how they'll exit both in profit and in loss.

3. The Art of Entry Buying Strategically

Buying a stock isn't about predicting it's about timing probabilities.

For penny stocks, price movements can be sharp and emotional. The key is to avoid chasing instead, wait for confirmation signals:

- Look for **breakouts** with strong volume. A stock breaking above a key resistance level with higher-than-average volume often indicates genuine investor interest.
- Avoid sudden spikes without volume support these are often pump-and-dump traps.
- Enter gradually. Instead of buying all at once, consider **phased entries** for example, 50% at your target level, 25% if it dips slightly, and 25% if it breaks higher. This reduces risk and smooths your cost basis.

Your goal isn't to buy at the absolute bottom it's to buy within a rational, risk-managed zone. Remember, professionals don't aim to be perfect; they aim to be consistent.

4. Managing Open Positions

Once you've bought, your work isn't done. In fact, this is where most traders make mistakes they stop managing and start hoping.

To trade like a pro, you must:

- Monitor volume, price movement, and any new catalysts daily.
- Adjust your stop-loss upwards when your stock moves favorably a technique called **trailing stop**. It locks in profit while allowing room for further upside.
- Keep emotions neutral. Don't celebrate early gains or panic at normal dips. Penny stocks move fast; patience wins more than speed.

Create a simple trade journal to record why you entered, your targets, and what happened. Over time, your journal becomes your private teacher showing patterns in your success and mistakes.

5. Knowing When to Sell The Exit Strategy

Most traders obsess over entries but forget that **exits define profit.** Knowing when to sell is an art that blends analysis and self-discipline.

There are three primary sell signals:

1. **Target Hit:** When your price objective is reached, sell at least part of your position to lock in gains. Partial exits protect profits while leaving room for growth.
2. **Trend Breakdown:** If price falls below a key moving average (like the 50-day or 200-day EMA) or breaks support on high volume, it may be time to exit.
3. **Change in Fundamentals or News:** If earnings disappoint, promoters sell large chunks, or regulators raise red flags exit quickly. Your capital is your oxygen; never risk it on hope.

Professionals never let a winning trade turn into a loss. Even selling early and leaving some gains on the table is better than staying too long and watching profits vanish.

6. Paper Trading: Practice Before You Risk Real Money

Before trading live, every great trader practices. **Paper trading** or simulated trading allows you to test your strategies without financial risk.

Many platforms like TradingView, Webull, and Investopedia simulators let you place virtual trades in real markets. Use this phase to:

- Practice identifying setups and executing orders.
- Build emotional discipline without pressure.
- Refine your risk-reward ratio and position sizing.

Treat your paper trading seriously as if it were real money. The habits you build here will follow you into real markets.

7. The Professional Mindset: Process Over Profit

The real difference between pros and amateurs lies in mindset. Amateurs chase outcomes; professionals master the process.

Trading isn't a one-time event it's a lifelong discipline of execution, review, and refinement. Each trade teaches something new about markets and about yourself. The goal isn't to be right every time it's to be profitable over time.

Remember:

> In penny stocks, even a 40% win rate can make you wealthy if your winners are much larger than your losers. It's not about accuracy; it's about asymmetry.

By applying these principles structured preparation, controlled entries, disciplined exits, and emotional neutrality you'll trade like a professional, even if you're just starting out.

This is the bridge between theory and mastery. Once you've internalized these steps, you'll no longer feel like you're reacting to markets you'll feel like you're orchestrating them.

6.2 Intraday, Swing, and Long Term Approaches

Investing in penny stocks isn't just about *what* you buy it's about *how* you trade. Every investor needs a clear time horizon and strategy whether you aim to make money in hours, weeks, or years. The difference between an amateur and a professional often lies not in the stock picked, but in the **approach and discipline** used to manage it.

This section explores three dominant trading styles **Intraday**, **Swing**, and **Long-Term Investing** each with its own rhythm, psychology, and payoff potential.

Intraday Trading The Art of Fast Decisions

What It Is

Intraday trading, also called **day trading**, involves buying and selling a stock on the same day capitalizing on small price movements within hours or even minutes. The goal is not to hold positions overnight; every trade begins and ends before the market closes.

Why Penny Stocks Are Attractive Here

Penny stocks exhibit extreme volatility and for intraday traders, **volatility is opportunity**. A small move in price can represent large percentage gains. For example, a INR 20 stock rising to INR 22 is a 10% gain in one day something large-cap stocks rarely achieve.

Core Principles

- **Liquidity is King:** Only trade penny stocks with sufficient daily volume ideally above 500,000 shares per day.
- **Use Tight Stop-Losses:** A strict stop-loss at 2–3% below entry price prevents small losses from becoming catastrophic.
- **Follow Momentum, Not Emotions:** Use VWAP and RSI to identify short-term strength and weakness.
- **Never Chase:** If you miss an entry, let it go. Chasing leads to buying at tops and selling at bottoms.

Tools & Techniques

- **Charts:** 1-minute, 5-minute, and 15-minute timeframes.
- **Indicators:** VWAP, MACD, RSI, Bollinger Bands.
- **Platforms:** Webull, TradingView, Zerodha Kite.

Who It's For

Traders with fast decision-making skills, high discipline, and the ability to monitor markets for hours. Intraday trading is thrilling and risky like surfing volatile waves of market momentum.

Swing Trading The Bridge Between Speed and Strategy

What It Is

Swing trading captures medium-term movements typically lasting from a few days to several weeks. It aims to profit from **trend waves** driven by earnings, news, or sector momentum.

Why Penny Stocks Shine for Swing Traders

Penny stocks often trend sharply after catalysts such as new contracts or approvals. For example, a INR 12 stock rising to INR 18 in two weeks delivers a 50% gain ideal for swing traders.

Core Principles

- Identify **strong technical setups** breakout zones with increasing volume.
- Use **trend indicators:** 20-day and 50-day moving averages, MACD crossovers, and RSI.
- Define **profit targets (15–30%)** and **stop-losses (5–10%)** before entry.
- Track **corporate and industry news** closely many swings are news-driven.

Advantages

- Less stressful than intraday trading.
- Time for research and reflection.
- Ideal for professionals who can monitor markets part-time.

Risks

- Overnight gaps due to unexpected news.
- Sudden sell-offs in illiquid stocks.

Who It's For

Individuals seeking balance between short-term excitement and medium-term strategy. Swing trading combines patience with agility ideal for steady compounding.

Long-Term Investing The Real Wealth Builder

What It Is

Long-term investing involves holding penny or small-cap stocks for months or years, betting on a company's transformation rather than short-term price moves. Here, you invest in the **business**, not just the ticker.

Why It Works

Many historical multibaggers started as penny stocks. Examples include:

- **Titan Company (India)** a micro-cap in the 1990s, now a blue-chip.
- **Monster Beverage (USA)** traded below $1 in the early 2000s, later rose over 100,000%.

Core Principles

- Focus on **fundamentals:** earnings growth, debt, cash flow, and management quality.
- **Diversify intelligently:** 10–15 stocks across industries.
- **Ride secular themes:** AI, renewable energy, healthcare, defense, or EVs.
- Practice **patience:** stay invested through volatility.

Advantages

- Builds long-term wealth.
- Compounds returns through reinvestment.
- Requires minimal daily monitoring.

Risks

- Market cycles and economic downturns.
- Possible delisting or dilution in weak firms.

Who It's For

Investors with a long-term mindset and conviction in business growth. Long-term investing transforms speculation into sustainable wealth creation.

Choosing Your Strategy

No approach is universally best. Each suits a different personality and objective.

Approach	Time Horizon	Skill	Risk	Gain Target	Ideal For
Intraday	Minutes Hours	High	Very High	1–5% daily	Fast, active traders
Swing	Days Weeks	Moderate	Medium	10–30% per trade	Working professionals
Long-Term	Months Years	High (research)	Medium High	200–1000%	Patient investors

Blended Strategies The Smart Investor's Edge

Many successful investors blend strategies:

- Use intraday or swing profits to fund long-term positions.
- Keep a core portfolio for compounding, while actively trading short-term opportunities.

This hybrid approach allows flexibility *earning today while investing in tomorrow.*

Final Thoughts

Whether you chase short-term gains or build long-term wealth, success comes from **self-awareness, structure, and discipline**. The right approach isn't the one promising the highest returns it's the one you can execute consistently. The best traders aren't fortune-tellers; they're **probability managers** who master one method, stay disciplined, and let compounding do the rest.

6.3 Paper Trading Exercises and Simulation Apps to Minimize Risk

Before risking a single dollar or rupee in the markets, every successful trader learns one fundamental truth: **Practice beats prediction.**

Paper trading or simulated trading allows you to learn, test, and refine your strategies without putting real money at risk. It is the financial world's version of a flight simulator: safe, realistic, and designed to prepare you for the real turbulence of live markets.

What is Paper Trading?

Paper trading is the process of making virtual trades using live market data, but without actual capital involved. You track your hypothetical positions as if they were real buying, selling, setting stop-losses, and recording profits or losses.

The term originated before computers, when traders literally recorded hypothetical trades on paper to test ideas. Today, sophisticated simulation platforms let you experience the full trading process from order execution to portfolio tracking in real time.

In essence:

- You practice trading in a **zero-risk environment**.
- You learn the **mechanics of order placement**.
- You build **discipline and emotional control** before entering real markets.

Why Paper Trading Matters

Many traders underestimate the complexity of executing a trade. They focus on finding "winning stocks," but ignore the mechanics timing entries, exits, and managing emotions. Paper trading helps bridge this gap by allowing you to:

1. **Understand Platform Tools:** Get familiar with the user interface, charts, and order types (market, limit, stop-loss).

2. **Develop Confidence:** When you know how your strategy behaves, you trade with clarity, not fear.

3. **Identify Weaknesses:** Paper trading reveals flaws in your system risky setups, poor timing, or unrealistic expectations.

4. **Test Risk Management Rules:** Apply stop-losses, diversification, and position sizing in a simulated environment before risking capital.

Paper trading, however, is not just a beginner's tool. Even professionals use simulation accounts to test **new strategies**, backtest **algorithmic models**, or study **market reactions to news events**. It's not a sign of inexperience it's a sign of discipline.

Popular Paper Trading Platforms

Different markets and regions offer unique tools for simulation. Below are some of the most trusted global platforms that support realistic paper trading.

- **TradingView:** A global favorite among retail and professional traders. Offers live data, charting tools, and "Paper Trading Mode" integrated directly into the platform. You can simulate real trades with virtual funds.

- **Webull Paper Trading (US, Global):** Ideal for beginners. Offers a mobile-friendly interface with real-time US market data and $1,000,000 in virtual cash.

- **TD Ameritrade ThinkorSwim (US):** A professional-grade simulator with advanced tools for technical and options traders.

- **Interactive Brokers Demo (Global):** Provides access to multiple exchanges worldwide and realistic execution simulations perfect for serious investors.

- **Zerodha Varsity and Kite (India):** Though Zerodha doesn't have an official simulator, many traders use demo environments or connect TradingView for paper trading Indian stocks.

- **Trading 212 Practice Account (UK, Europe):** Offers zero-risk paper trading with live market conditions and virtual balance a good start for European users.

Setting Up Your Paper Trading Journey

To get the most value out of paper trading, approach it systematically not as casual play, but as a structured training program. Here's a step-by-step plan:

1. **Set a Virtual Budget:** Decide how much "virtual money" represents your real investment capacity. If you can only afford $500 in real life, practice with the same amount virtually.
2. **Define Goals:** What are you testing intraday setups, swing trading, or long-term entries? Each requires different timeframes and analysis.
3. **Create a Trading Journal:** Record every trade reason for entry, stop-loss, target, result, and emotional state. This builds accountability.
4. **Simulate Real Conditions:** Trade at actual market hours, avoid "rewind testing," and don't adjust stop-losses after the fact. Treat it as real money.
5. **Review Weekly Performance:** Identify recurring mistakes chasing breakouts, overtrading, ignoring risk limits and refine your approach.

Emotional Discipline The Hidden Lesson

The biggest difference between paper trading and real trading is emotion. When no real money is at stake, traders tend to take excessive risks or skip stop-losses. To make paper trading effective, you must simulate not only trades, but also the **psychology of risk**.

Pro Tip: When paper trading, imagine every loss reduces your real savings and every gain is money you've earned through effort. This mental framing helps you develop emotional resilience.

From Simulation to Real Markets

The goal of paper trading isn't to stay in simulation forever it's to transition confidently into the real market. Once you achieve consistent virtual performance say, 3–6 months of steady, profitable results it's time to move forward.

Before Going Live, Ensure You:

- Have a **tested strategy** with clear entry and exit criteria.
- Understand your platform's order types and fees.
- Are comfortable with risk per trade (usually 1–2% of total capital).
- Accept that losses will happen even the best traders lose often, but manage losses intelligently.

Sample Exercise Plan

Here's a sample structure to train effectively over four weeks:

Week	Focus Area and Objectives
Week 1	Learn platform basics placing orders, setting stop-losses, monitoring charts. Make 10 paper trades to understand execution.
Week 2	Test intraday and swing setups using indicators like RSI and moving averages. Focus on timing entries and exits.
Week 3	Simulate risk management apply fixed position sizes and max loss per day. Start maintaining a detailed journal.
Week 4	Evaluate total performance, identify your edge, and adjust strategy. Prepare to transition toward small real trades.

Final Thoughts

Paper trading is the **foundation of real-world trading success.** It teaches you to analyze data, control emotions, and respect the process before money ever changes hands. Many of today's elite traders began by losing fake money and learning priceless lessons.

In trading, *the market always gives the exam first and the lesson later.* Paper trading reverses that order it gives you the lessons before the exam. So practice wisely, document everything, and step into the real market only when your skills not luck are ready to perform.

Key Takeaways

1. **Trading is a discipline, not a gamble.** Successful traders follow structured strategies, predefined risk rules, and emotional control not random hunches or impulsive decisions. Every trade is part of a larger system that compounds consistency, not luck.

2. **Understand the three major trading styles.**

   - **Intraday trading:** Focuses on quick, same-day moves, capitalizing on volatility and momentum. It requires precision, speed, and emotional stability.
   - **Swing trading:** Captures medium-term price swings lasting from days to weeks, balancing time commitment with higher accuracy.
   - **Long-term investing:** Builds wealth through compounding, patience, and conviction the opposite of chasing trends.

3. **Choose a strategy that fits your personality and time.** Not everyone thrives in high-speed intraday trading or has the patience

for multi-year holding. Align your method with your temperament, availability, and risk tolerance. Your success depends on *fit*, not fashion.

4. **The entry is easy but exit defines profit.** Most traders obsess over buying, yet the real art lies in when and how to sell. A planned exit strategy whether stop-loss, target-based, or trailing separates disciplined traders from emotional ones.

5. **Risk management is your real edge.** Never risk more than 1–2% of your capital on a single trade. Use stop-loss orders, position sizing, and diversification to survive drawdowns. The best traders focus on *staying in the game*, not just winning one round.

6. **Paper trading is your safest training ground.** Before putting real money at stake, practice with simulation apps such as TradingView, Webull Paper, or the Investopedia Simulator. Treat it seriously set rules, review trades, and build consistency before going live.

7. **Master trade journaling and reflection.** Every trade should teach you something. Track your reasoning, emotions, and results to identify patterns what works, what doesn't, and how to evolve. Your trade journal is your most powerful teacher.

8. **Tools matter but mindset matters more.** While advanced platforms, screeners, and charts help identify opportunities, your real competitive advantage lies in discipline, patience, and adaptability.

9. **Consistency beats complexity.** You don't need a dozen indicators or a secret algorithm just one strategy executed flawlessly over time. Traders who survive and thrive are those who trade less, think clearly, and adapt fast.

10. **Every great trader was once a beginner.** The pros you admire started small, made mistakes, and learned through experience. With structured practice, journaling, and self-awareness, you can move from guessing to mastering and trade like a true professional.

Chapter 7

Market Mechanics Uncovered

Behind every flashing price ticker and trading screen lies a living, breathing ecosystem of players, probabilities, and psychology. Most new investors see only numbers rising and falling but beneath those numbers are powerful forces shaping how markets move, react, and evolve. Understanding these invisible mechanics is what separates a casual trader from a market professional.

Every transaction whether buying a penny stock, a blue-chip, or an ETF is driven by a delicate balance of **liquidity**, **bid-ask spreads**, and **volatility**. These are not abstract terms; they define the very structure of opportunity and risk. When liquidity dries up, even the best stock can fall sharply. When spreads widen, your profit margins shrink before you even begin. And when volatility spikes, fortunes can be made or lost in minutes.

In this chapter, we'll journey beneath the surface of market prices to uncover what really drives them. You'll learn:

- How **bid-ask spreads** work and why small differences matter, especially in penny stocks and thinly traded assets.
- What **liquidity** means in practical terms how it affects entry, exit, and slippage and how to identify truly tradable opportunities.
- The role of **market makers, insiders, and promoters** who influence prices and flow behind the scenes sometimes stabilizing markets, sometimes manipulating them.
- How to read **volume patterns, price charts, and technical indicators** not as predictions, but as signals of crowd behavior and probability.

Think of this chapter as your backstage pass to the financial theater. Here, you'll see how markets are constructed, how orders interact, and how emotions become numbers on a screen. Once you understand these hidden mechanisms, you'll trade not with blind faith but with clarity, context, and control.

The goal is not just to understand how the market works, but how to use that knowledge to protect yourself from traps, identify real momentum, and build conviction in every decision you make. Whether you're analyzing a penny stock or a global index, the mechanics are universal and mastering them is your foundation for sustainable success.

7.1 Bid-Ask Spreads, Liquidity, and Volatility Explained

Every trade in the financial markets, from small penny stocks to large-cap equities, is influenced by three fundamental mechanics: **bid-ask spreads**, **liquidity**, and **volatility**. These elements shape not only the cost of entering and exiting positions but also the opportunities and risks you face as an investor or trader. Understanding them is essential for building a disciplined, professional approach to the markets.

Bid-Ask Spread: Understanding the Hidden Cost

The **bid price** is the maximum price a buyer is willing to pay for a stock, while the **ask price** is the minimum a seller will accept. The difference between these prices is called the **spread**.

- In highly liquid, large-cap stocks, spreads are usually very narrow often just a few cents or fractions of a rupee. This means entering or exiting a position comes at minimal cost.
- In low-liquidity markets, such as many penny stocks, spreads can widen significantly. A wide spread effectively increases your cost immediately upon buying, and reduces potential gains when selling.
- Spreads are influenced by supply and demand, trading volume, and the presence of market makers. Understanding spreads helps traders evaluate transaction costs and avoid hidden losses.

Key takeaway: Always check the spread before entering a trade. Narrow spreads signal healthy liquidity, while wide spreads require caution.

Liquidity: The Flow of the Market

Liquidity measures how easily an asset can be bought or sold without affecting its price. It is a critical factor in determining your ability to enter and exit trades smoothly.

- Highly liquid stocks allow large transactions with minimal price impact. Low-liquidity stocks, often penny stocks, can experience dramatic price swings even on small trades.
- Liquidity is impacted by market capitalization, trading volume, and investor interest. Stocks with low daily volume are harder to trade and carry higher risk.
- Liquidity also affects slippage the difference between the expected price of a trade and the price at which it is executed. In illiquid markets, slippage can be substantial.

Key takeaway: Evaluate a stock's liquidity before investing. Thinly traded stocks require careful position sizing and timing.

Volatility: Measuring Market Movement

Volatility refers to the degree of price fluctuations over time. It is a double-edged sword: the same volatility that can generate massive profits can also cause significant losses.

- **Low-volatility stocks** tend to move gradually, suitable for conservative or long-term investors.
- **High-volatility stocks** fluctuate rapidly, offering trading opportunities but increasing risk. Penny stocks often exhibit extreme volatility, moving 20–50% in a single session due to news, sentiment, or thin liquidity.
- Traders can quantify volatility using metrics like the Average True Range (ATR) or standard deviation. These indicators help assess potential risk and set realistic targets and stop-losses.

Key takeaway: Understanding volatility allows you to anticipate price swings, plan risk management, and avoid being caught off guard.

Interconnection of Bid-Ask, Liquidity, and Volatility

These three mechanics are deeply intertwined:

- Low liquidity often causes wider spreads and higher volatility.
- High volatility increases trading risk, even in moderately liquid stocks.
- Narrow spreads combined with high liquidity generally create a safer and more predictable trading environment.

Traders who master these concepts can better evaluate market opportunities and identify risk before committing capital. A deep understanding of bid-ask spreads, liquidity, and volatility transforms trading from guessing into calculated probability-based decisions.

Practical Insights for Traders

1. Always review the bid-ask spread before entering a trade, especially in penny stocks.
2. Check the stock's trading volume and liquidity to ensure you can enter and exit positions without large slippage.
3. Measure volatility to gauge potential price swings and adjust your position size, targets, and stop-losses accordingly.
4. Integrate all three elements into your trading plan to make informed, high-probability decisions.

By consistently applying these principles, you build a strong foundation for trading or investing in any market whether you're navigating penny stocks, small-caps, or blue-chip equities. Knowledge of these mechanics allows you to approach the market with confidence, discipline, and strategic insight.

7.2 Roles of Promoters, Insiders, and Market Makers

In any financial market, prices do not move randomly. Behind every trade are participants who influence supply, demand, and investor behavior. Three key actors play a pivotal role in the price dynamics of stocks, particularly in penny stocks and small-cap markets: **promoters**, **insiders**, and **market makers**. Understanding their roles is essential for trading strategically and avoiding common pitfalls.

Promoters: Architects of a Company's Direction

Promoters are individuals or entities responsible for starting, funding, and guiding a company. They hold significant influence over strategic decisions and can substantially impact a stock's market behavior.

- **Ownership and Control:** Promoters typically retain a significant percentage of shares, giving them control over board decisions, company strategy, and sometimes even stock issuance.
- **Stock Issuance and Capital Raising:** Promoters often lead IPOs or private funding rounds, which can influence stock price and investor perception.
- **Impact on Market Sentiment:** Large purchases or sales by promoters can create momentum in the stock, signaling confidence or caution to the market.

Key Insight: Monitoring promoter activity helps traders gauge confidence in the company's long-term prospects. In low-liquidity markets, such as penny stocks, these moves can dramatically affect prices.

Insiders: Knowledgeable Participants

Insiders include executives, directors, and employees with access to non-public, material information. Their transactions and behavior can be leading indicators for price movements.

- **Insider Buying:** Often interpreted as a sign of confidence in the company's future performance.
- **Insider Selling:** Can indicate personal financial needs, loss of confidence, or strategic repositioning.
- **Regulatory Compliance:** Most exchanges require insiders to report trades, ensuring transparency for investors.

Key Insight: Patterns of insider activity, while not guarantees, can provide valuable signals for potential stock movements.

Market Makers: Facilitators of Liquidity

Market makers are professionals who provide liquidity by continuously quoting buy (bid) and sell (ask) prices. They ensure that other participants can trade without waiting for a counterparty.

- **Role in Trading:** By buying and selling, market makers reduce the risk of price gaps and enable smoother market operations.
- **Profit from Spreads:** They earn from the difference between bid and ask prices. In illiquid stocks, this spread can be substantial.
- **Influence on Prices:** While generally stabilizing, market makers in low-volume stocks can contribute to sharp price swings.

Key Insight: Awareness of market maker activity helps traders avoid unexpected slippage or sudden price movements, particularly in penny stocks.

The Interplay Between Promoters, Insiders, and Market Makers

- Promoters and insiders influence perception and confidence in a stock, setting the stage for market behavior.
- Market makers translate these perceptions into executable trades, providing liquidity but sometimes amplifying short-term price swings.
- Understanding how these actors interact allows traders to anticipate potential opportunities and risks.

Practical Applications for Traders

1. Track changes in promoter and insider holdings to detect confidence or caution signals.

2. Observe regulatory filings and announcements to understand insider intentions.

3. Consider the role of market makers in low-liquidity markets to plan trade sizes and entry/exit timing.

4. Combine insights from promoters, insiders, and market makers with technical and fundamental analysis for higher-probability trades.

By mastering the roles of promoters, insiders, and market makers, traders gain a deeper understanding of how price movements occur, especially in penny stocks and small-cap markets. This knowledge allows for informed, disciplined, and strategic investing.

7.3 Reading Charts, Volume, and Technical Indicators Effectively

Technical analysis is a critical skill for traders seeking to understand market behavior, spot opportunities, and manage risk. Charts, trading volume, and technical indicators provide a visual and mathematical representation of market activity. Mastering these tools enables traders to make informed decisions rather than relying on guesswork or emotion.

Understanding Stock Charts

Stock charts graphically display a stock's price movement over time. They are the foundation of technical analysis and come in several forms:

- **Line Charts:** Connect closing prices over a time period, offering a clear view of trends and direction. Ideal for beginners.

- **Bar Charts:** Show open, high, low, and close (OHLC) prices for each time period. Useful for analyzing price range and volatility.

- **Candlestick Charts:** Each candle represents OHLC data with color-coded bullish (green/white) or bearish (red/black) movements. Candlesticks reveal patterns that can signal reversals or continuations.

Key Insight: Learn to read candlestick patterns, as they provide rich information about investor sentiment and short-term price direction.

The Importance of Trading Volume

Volume measures the number of shares traded in a given time period and indicates market activity:

- High volume confirms the strength of a price move. A breakout with strong volume is more likely to sustain than one on low volume.
- Low volume can indicate a lack of conviction, increasing the likelihood of false breakouts or reversals.
- Volume spikes often precede volatility, providing clues for potential trading opportunities.

Key Insight: Always analyze price movement in conjunction with volume. A rising stock on declining volume may signal weakening momentum, while falling stocks on high volume can indicate panic selling.

Technical Indicators: Adding Analytical Depth

Technical indicators are mathematical calculations based on price and volume data. They help identify trends, momentum, and potential reversal points:

- **Moving Averages (MA):** Smooth out price data to reveal trends. Common types include the 50-day and 200-day moving averages.
- **Relative Strength Index (RSI):** Measures the speed and change of price movements, indicating overbought or oversold conditions.
- **Moving Average Convergence Divergence (MACD):** Shows trend direction and momentum, signaling potential buy or sell points.
- **Bollinger Bands:** Plot volatility bands around a moving average, helping identify overextended prices and potential reversals.
- **Support and Resistance Levels:** Key price levels where the stock historically struggles to move below (support) or above (resistance).

Key Insight: Indicators should complement, not replace, price and volume analysis. Multiple indicators together can provide higher confidence in trading signals.

Combining Charts, Volume, and Indicators

Successful traders integrate these tools:

1. Identify the trend using charts and moving averages.
2. Confirm the trend with volume analysis.

3. Use indicators like RSI, MACD, and Bollinger Bands to fine-tune entry and exit points.
4. Look for convergence: price movement, volume, and indicator signals aligning to increase trade probability.
5. Continuously validate patterns with historical data and market context.

Practical Tips for Effective Technical Analysis

- Always start with a clean chart, free of unnecessary indicators.
- Focus on a few key indicators that suit your trading style to avoid analysis paralysis.
- Backtest strategies using historical data or paper trading before risking real capital.
- Consider multiple timeframes (daily, weekly, intraday) to gain a comprehensive view.
- Stay aware of news, events, and macroeconomic factors that may override technical signals.

By mastering charts, volume, and technical indicators, traders gain a significant edge. These tools translate raw market activity into actionable insights, allowing you to navigate volatility, identify high-probability trades, and manage risk effectively. Combined with fundamental analysis, this knowledge equips you to make informed, disciplined, and strategic trading decisions in penny stocks, small-caps, and beyond.

Key Takeaways

- **Charts are foundational:** Line, bar, and candlestick charts provide visual insight into price movements and trends.
- **Volume confirms strength:** Analyze trading volume alongside price to differentiate between strong moves and potential false breakouts.
- **Indicators complement analysis:** Moving averages, RSI, MACD, and Bollinger Bands help identify trends, momentum, and potential reversals.
- **Combine tools for higher confidence:** Use charts, volume, and multiple indicators together to increase the probability of successful trades.
- **Support and resistance matter:** Recognize key price levels where the stock has historically struggled to move, which can guide entry and exit points.

- **Backtesting reduces risk:** Test strategies on historical data or paper trading platforms before committing real capital.
- **Timeframe awareness:** Consider multiple timeframes (intraday, daily, weekly) to get a holistic view of the market trend.
- **Context is key:** Always account for news, macroeconomic factors, and market sentiment, as these can override technical signals.
- **Discipline and focus:** Avoid cluttering charts with too many indicators; focus on what aligns with your trading strategy and risk tolerance.

Conclusion: Mastering charts, volume, and technical indicators transforms raw market data into actionable insights. Coupled with fundamental understanding, this knowledge equips traders to navigate markets with confidence, anticipate opportunities, and manage risks effectively, particularly in volatile and small-cap stocks.

Part III

Research, Screening & Analysis

Chapter 8

Fundamental Analysis Mastery

Fundamental analysis is the cornerstone of identifying high-potential investments. While technical analysis helps you understand market sentiment and price movements, fundamental analysis allows you to evaluate the intrinsic value of a company. For penny stocks, this is especially crucial: the right company can grow exponentially, but the wrong choice can quickly erode your capital.

This chapter will equip you with the tools to analyze companies systematically, focusing on financial health, growth potential, and sector dynamics. By the end, you will be able to screen and select penny stocks with strong underlying fundamentals rather than relying on hype or speculation.

Why Fundamental Analysis Matters for Penny Stocks

Penny stocks are inherently risky due to low liquidity, limited public information, and high volatility. Fundamental analysis helps you:

- **Separate solid opportunities from speculative hype:** Evaluate whether a low-priced stock has real growth potential.
- **Understand financial health:** Examine balance sheets, debt, and promoter holdings to assess stability and governance.
- **Measure growth potential:** Analyze earnings, dividends, and sector trends to identify long-term multibagger candidates.

Screening High-Potential Penny Stocks

Before investing, it is essential to filter and shortlist candidates based on key quantitative and qualitative metrics. This approach reduces guesswork and focuses your time on stocks with real multibagger potential.

- Financial ratios and key metrics to evaluate strength.
- Industry trends to identify sectors with growth tailwinds.
- Historical performance to assess track record and promoter credibility.

Sector-Specific Considerations

Certain sectors are more likely to produce multibagger returns due to innovation, regulatory support, or market expansion. In this chapter, we explore:

- **Artificial Intelligence (AI):** Rapid technological adoption and increasing enterprise spending.
- **Electric Vehicles (EV):** Transition from fossil fuels, government incentives, and global demand.
- **Renewable Energy:** Solar, wind, and green infrastructure benefiting from environmental policies.
- **Pharma and Healthcare:** Rising global demand for medicines, vaccines, and diagnostics.
- **Defence and Aerospace:** Strategic investments, government spending, and high barriers to entry.
- **Nuclear and Energy Infrastructure:** Long-term projects with significant growth potential.

What You Will Learn in This Chapter

By combining these principles, you will be able to:

- Perform rigorous financial analysis to identify fundamentally strong penny stocks.
- Interpret key metrics like debt, book value, and promoter holdings.
- Evaluate dividends, earnings, and sector trends to forecast growth potential.
- Apply sector-specific insights to increase the likelihood of selecting future multibaggers.

With a solid understanding of fundamental analysis, you will have the knowledge and confidence to separate true opportunities from noise, and build a systematic approach to long-term wealth creation through penny stocks.

8.1 Screening High-Potential Penny Stocks

Investing in penny stocks can feel like navigating a minefield: the prices are low, the potential upside can be enormous, but the risks are equally significant. The key to success is not random picking, hype, or speculation—it is a disciplined, structured screening process. This section guides you through the art and science of identifying penny stocks that have real multibagger potential.

Why Screening is Crucial

Penny stocks are typically companies with low market capitalization and limited trading volume. They are often under the radar, lacking analyst coverage, and subject to high volatility. A systematic screening approach allows you to:

- **Reduce Exposure to Weak Companies:** Avoid companies with poor governance, unsustainable debt, or inconsistent financials.
- **Save Time and Focus Resources:** Narrow hundreds of potential stocks to a manageable shortlist of high-probability candidates.
- **Identify True Growth Potential:** Focus on companies that demonstrate strong fundamentals and sector tailwinds.
- **Mitigate Emotional Decision-Making:** A structured framework reduces impulsive investments driven by fear, greed, or hype.

Core Screening Criteria

Successful screening combines quantitative and qualitative factors. Key considerations include:

1. **Market Capitalization and Liquidity:** Ensure the company has sufficient daily trading volume. Extremely illiquid stocks are difficult to enter or exit without moving the market.
2. **Financial Health:** Examine balance sheets for debt levels, cash reserves, and profitability. Companies with consistent revenue growth and positive cash flow are more likely to survive volatility.
3. **Promoter and Management Credibility:** High promoter ownership often indicates alignment with shareholder interests. Evaluate past track records, integrity, and management stability.
4. **Book Value and Asset Quality:** Stocks trading below book value may have hidden potential—but only if the underlying assets are sound and properly accounted for.

5. **Earnings and Revenue Trends:** Look for consistent growth in earnings and revenues over multiple quarters or years. Sudden spikes without underlying fundamentals are warning signs.

6. **Sector Dynamics:** Identify industries with growth tailwinds, such as AI, EVs, renewable energy, healthcare, or defense. A promising sector amplifies stock growth potential.

7. **Dividend and Return Metrics:** Even small dividends, positive return on equity (ROE), or return on assets (ROA) suggest financial discipline and shareholder focus.

Screening Tools and Resources

Today's digital tools make it possible to screen hundreds of stocks efficiently:

- **Screener.in (India):** Filter companies by revenue, profit, debt, promoter holdings, and more.
- **Finviz (U.S.):** Screen penny stocks by price, volume, market capitalization, sector, and key technical indicators.
- **TradingView / Moneycontrol:** Apply advanced filters and monitor sector performance, trading volume, and stock-specific metrics.

Step-by-Step Screening Process

A practical approach to screening:

1. **Define Investment Universe:** Set price, market capitalization, and sector boundaries.
2. **Apply Financial Filters:** Check for debt ratios, profitability, and cash flow.
3. **Assess Management:** Examine promoter holdings, board composition, and past performance.
4. **Shortlist Sector Leaders:** Focus on companies in sectors with strong growth trends or government support.
5. **Analyze Historical Trends and News:** Look at past price action, earnings, and corporate announcements to ensure transparency.

Common Screening Mistakes to Avoid

- **Chasing Low Prices:** A low share price alone does not make a stock valuable.

- **Ignoring Sector Context:** Even a fundamentally strong company may struggle if its sector is declining.
- **Overreliance on Promotions or Tips:** Avoid social media hype or unverified recommendations.
- **Neglecting Liquidity:** Insufficient trading volume can trap your capital in illiquid stocks.

Key Takeaways

- Screening is essential to identify fundamentally strong, high-potential penny stocks.
- Use a combination of market cap, financial metrics, management quality, and sector trends.
- Leverage digital tools and platforms to filter, analyze, and prioritize candidates.
- A systematic approach minimizes risk, reduces emotional decision-making, and increases the likelihood of discovering future multibaggers.

By mastering the screening process, you lay the foundation for informed investing in penny stocks. This disciplined approach transforms speculation into strategic decision-making, allowing you to focus on companies with genuine growth potential while mitigating unnecessary risk.

8.2 Key Financial Metrics: Balance Sheets, Debt, Promoter Holdings, Book Value

Understanding a company's financials is the cornerstone of fundamental analysis. For penny stocks, this knowledge becomes even more critical because these companies often operate with tighter margins, limited public scrutiny, and higher volatility. This section breaks down the key financial metrics that every serious investor should analyze before committing capital.

Balance Sheets: The Financial Snapshot

A balance sheet provides a snapshot of a company's financial position at a given point in time. It summarizes what the company owns (assets), owes (liabilities), and the shareholders' equity. For penny stocks, focus on:

- **Current Assets:** Cash, receivables, and inventories. Adequate liquidity ensures the company can meet short-term obligations.
- **Current Liabilities:** Short-term debts, payables, and other obligations. Compare with current assets to assess solvency.

- **Equity:** The net worth owned by shareholders. High equity relative to debt indicates stability and lower financial risk.
- **Asset Quality:** Verify that assets are tangible, correctly valued, and not over-inflated or obsolete.

A healthy balance sheet signals financial stability and the capacity to weather market volatility—especially important for companies trading at low prices.

Debt: Understanding Leverage and Risk

Debt can magnify returns but also magnify losses. When analyzing penny stocks:

- **Debt-to-Equity Ratio:** Measures the proportion of debt relative to shareholder equity. Lower ratios generally indicate safer investments.
- **Interest Coverage Ratio:** Ability of a company to pay interest from operating income. High coverage suggests the company can comfortably service debt.
- **Short-Term vs Long-Term Debt:** Short-term obligations require immediate liquidity, while long-term debt can be managed strategically.

Companies with manageable debt and strong cash flow are more likely to grow sustainably and avoid distress scenarios that can devastate investors.

Promoter and Insider Holdings

Promoters and insiders play a critical role in small-cap and penny stocks:

- **High Promoter Holding:** Indicates confidence and alignment of interests with shareholders.
- **Insider Transactions:** Monitor buying or selling by promoters, directors, or key executives. Frequent selling might signal red flags.
- **Management Credibility:** Evaluate past performance, ethical conduct, and strategic decisions. Credible leadership can drive long-term growth.

Insider alignment and transparency are key predictors of future stock performance, particularly in less-regulated penny stock markets.

Book Value: Assessing Intrinsic Worth

Book value represents the net value of a company's assets minus liabilities. It is a baseline measure of intrinsic value:

- **Price-to-Book (P/B) Ratio:** Compares market price to book value. Stocks trading below book value may be undervalued, but investigate why.
- **Asset-Backed Valuation:** Ensure assets are real, usable, and not overstated on paper.
- **Growth vs Value:** Book value alone doesn't guarantee a multibagger—combine with earnings, sector potential, and market trends.

Integrating Metrics for Holistic Analysis

No single metric can determine a penny stock's quality. Effective investors integrate multiple data points:

- Balance sheets reveal liquidity and solvency.
- Debt metrics highlight financial leverage and risk exposure.
- Promoter and insider holdings show alignment and credibility.
- Book value provides a baseline for intrinsic worth.

By combining these metrics, you can shortlist fundamentally strong companies that are capable of sustainable growth and are more likely to become multibaggers over time.

Key Takeaways

- Analyze balance sheets for liquidity, solvency, and equity strength.
- Monitor debt levels and interest coverage to avoid over-leveraged companies.
- Evaluate promoter and insider holdings for alignment and credibility.
- Compare market price with book value to identify potential undervaluation.
- Integrate multiple metrics for a holistic understanding of a company's financial health before investing.

Mastering these key financial metrics equips you with the ability to separate strong, promising penny stocks from those that carry hidden risks. With this foundation, your investment decisions move from guesswork to strategic, informed analysis.

8.3 Dividends, Earnings, and Sector Growth Potential

Beyond balance sheets and financial ratios, understanding a company's cash generation and market positioning is critical when evaluating penny stocks. Dividends, earnings trends, and the growth potential of the sector in which a company operates provide vital clues about both stability and upside potential. This section explores these elements in detail, offering a framework for identifying penny stocks with genuine multibagger potential.

Dividends: Signaling Financial Discipline

Dividends are a direct return to shareholders and an indicator of financial health:

- **Dividend Yield:** The annual dividend divided by the stock price shows how much cash an investor earns relative to the investment. Even small yields indicate that a company generates enough profit to return value to shareholders.
- **Dividend Payout Ratio:** Percentage of earnings paid as dividends. Sustainable payout ratios (often below 50%) suggest that the company retains sufficient capital for growth while rewarding investors.
- **Consistency of Dividends:** Companies that maintain or gradually increase dividends over time demonstrate stability and disciplined financial management.

For penny stocks, a dividend is less common than in blue-chip companies, but spotting consistent or emerging dividend payers can indicate financial prudence, even in smaller companies.

Earnings: The Engine of Value Creation

Earnings are the lifeblood of a company and a primary driver of stock performance:

- **Revenue Growth:** Examine quarterly and annual revenue trends. Consistent growth indicates increasing market traction and demand for the company's products or services.
- **Profit Margins:** Analyze gross, operating, and net margins. Higher margins relative to peers suggest operational efficiency and pricing power.
- **Earnings Per Share (EPS):** Tracks profitability on a per-share basis. Rising EPS often correlates with stock price appreciation.

- **Earnings Stability vs Volatility:** Avoid companies with erratic earnings unless there is a clear reason for the fluctuation, such as seasonality or strategic investment.

For penny stocks, small absolute profits can be deceptive—what matters is the trajectory and the potential for compounding growth over time.

Sector Growth Potential: Riding the Tailwinds

The broader sector a company operates in significantly impacts its ability to become a multibagger:

- **Identify Growth Sectors:** Look for industries with strong secular trends, regulatory support, or technological disruption. Examples include AI, electric vehicles (EVs), renewable energy, pharmaceuticals, and defense.
- **Compare to Industry Peers:** A company growing faster than its peers in a high-growth sector is often positioned to capture market share and outperform.
- **Government Policies and Incentives:** Subsidies, tax benefits, or infrastructure investment can accelerate sector growth, providing tailwinds for companies in the space.
- **Global Market Opportunities:** Penny stocks with products or services that can scale internationally have higher multibagger potential.

Understanding the sector context helps investors differentiate between a company growing because of its fundamentals versus one benefiting solely from temporary hype.

Integrating Dividends, Earnings, and Sector Trends

A disciplined investor evaluates these elements together:

1. **Assess Earnings Quality:** Strong, consistent earnings are the foundation of long-term growth.
2. **Evaluate Dividends as a Confidence Signal:** Even modest payouts signal financial discipline and management confidence.
3. **Analyze Sector Momentum:** Growth sectors amplify the effect of strong earnings and prudent management.
4. **Look for Alignment:** Companies that combine good earnings, disciplined financial policies, and favorable sector dynamics are prime multibagger candidates.

Key Takeaways

- Dividends indicate financial discipline, even in small-cap or penny stocks.
- Consistent earnings and revenue growth are primary drivers of long-term stock appreciation.
- Sector growth potential can amplify the upside of fundamentally strong companies.
- Integrating dividends, earnings trends, and sector tailwinds provides a holistic framework for selecting high-potential penny stocks.

By mastering these metrics, you move beyond superficial stock selection and begin identifying companies with both strong internal financial health and the external market conditions necessary to achieve multibagger returns. This approach transforms your investing process into a strategic, research-driven discipline.

8.4 Sector-Specific Examples: AI, EV, Renewable Energy, Pharma, Defence, Nuclear

Understanding sector dynamics is crucial for identifying penny stocks with multibagger potential. Certain industries experience faster growth, higher innovation, or favorable regulatory tailwinds. By studying these sectors, investors can pinpoint companies that are positioned to benefit disproportionately from macro trends. This section explores six high-potential sectors with global relevance.

Artificial Intelligence (AI)

AI is transforming industries from healthcare to finance:

- **Growth Drivers:** Advancements in machine learning, data analytics, and cloud computing fuel demand for AI solutions.
- **Investment Opportunities:** Small-cap AI startups often innovate faster and take niche market positions, offering significant upside potential.
- **Risks:** High competition, rapid obsolescence, and regulatory scrutiny on data privacy.
- **Global Relevance:** AI adoption is not limited to a single geography; companies with scalable software solutions can target multiple markets.

Electric Vehicles (EVs)

The EV sector is in a structural growth phase:

- **Growth Drivers:** Government incentives, environmental regulations, and consumer shift to sustainable mobility.
- **Investment Opportunities:** Battery manufacturers, component suppliers, and EV startups often start as penny stocks but can scale rapidly.
- **Risks:** High capital intensity, evolving technology standards, and intense competition.
- **Global Relevance:** Demand is growing across North America, Europe, and Asia, making it a globally investable sector.

Renewable Energy

Clean energy is a long-term megatrend:

- **Growth Drivers:** Solar, wind, and bioenergy adoption is accelerating due to climate initiatives and energy security concerns.
- **Investment Opportunities:** Small renewable energy firms, especially in emerging markets, often trade at low valuations initially but can experience exponential growth.
- **Risks:** Regulatory dependency, project execution risk, and technological changes.
- **Global Relevance:** Energy transition is a worldwide phenomenon; companies with scalable technologies have global market potential.

Pharmaceuticals

Healthcare innovation remains a resilient sector:

- **Growth Drivers:** Aging populations, rising healthcare demand, and new drug discovery.
- **Investment Opportunities:** Small-cap biotech and pharmaceutical companies often hold patents or pipelines that can drive multibagger returns.
- **Risks:** Regulatory approvals, clinical trial failures, and intellectual property challenges.
- **Global Relevance:** Pharmaceutical innovations are globally distributed, and successful products often reach international markets.

Defence

Defence companies often benefit from strategic government contracts:

- **Growth Drivers:** Geopolitical tensions, modernization programs, and rising defense budgets.
- **Investment Opportunities:** Niche suppliers, technology integrators, and small-cap defense manufacturers can experience rapid valuation increases.
- **Risks:** Dependence on government contracts, regulatory compliance, and political risks.
- **Global Relevance:** Defense supply chains are increasingly international, creating opportunities beyond domestic markets.

Nuclear Energy

A sector often overlooked but with massive growth potential:

- **Growth Drivers:** Clean energy mandates, energy security, and technological advances in reactor design.
- **Investment Opportunities:** Small-cap firms in nuclear technology, fuel processing, and safety systems can see significant upside as the sector expands.
- **Risks:** Regulatory barriers, high initial capital costs, and public perception.
- **Global Relevance:** Nuclear power is critical for energy transition strategies worldwide, especially in Asia, Europe, and North America.

Integrating Sector Insights into Penny Stock Selection

Investors should combine sector analysis with company-specific fundamentals:

1. Identify sectors with strong long-term tailwinds.
2. Analyze which small-cap companies are positioned to capture the growth in these sectors.
3. Assess financial health, management credibility, and operational scalability.
4. Consider global market potential to evaluate the true upside.

Key Takeaways

- High-growth sectors amplify the potential returns of fundamentally strong penny stocks.
- AI, EV, renewable energy, pharmaceuticals, defense, and nuclear energy are sectors with global multibagger potential.
- Understanding sector-specific risks and opportunities is essential for disciplined investing.
- Combining sector trends with company-level financial analysis increases the probability of identifying multibagger opportunities.

By studying sector dynamics alongside company fundamentals, investors can systematically shortlist penny stocks that are not only undervalued but also positioned to ride powerful market tailwinds, increasing the odds of achieving substantial, long-term returns.

Key Takeaways

- High-growth sectors provide structural tailwinds that can significantly amplify the returns of fundamentally strong penny stocks.
- **Artificial Intelligence (AI):** Offers opportunities in software, data analytics, and automation with global scalability.
- **Electric Vehicles (EV):** Small-cap companies in batteries, components, and EV startups can grow rapidly with government incentives and rising demand.
- **Renewable Energy:** Solar, wind, and bioenergy firms, especially in emerging markets, can benefit from global energy transition trends.
- **Pharmaceuticals:** Biotech and pharma startups with patents or strong pipelines can generate multibagger returns through innovation.
- **Defence:** Niche suppliers and small manufacturers benefit from strategic contracts and modernization programs, though political and regulatory risks exist.
- **Nuclear Energy:** Emerging nuclear technology companies can gain from global clean energy mandates and energy security initiatives.
- Integrating sector analysis with company fundamentals (earnings, financial health, management quality) increases the probability of identifying true multibagger candidates.
- Understanding global opportunities ensures that investments are not limited by geography, maximizing potential upside.

By focusing on sector tailwinds and combining them with rigorous fundamental analysis, investors can create a structured approach to identify high-potential penny stocks with significant long-term growth prospects.

Chapter 9

Technical Analysis Mastery

Technical analysis is a cornerstone of trading and investing, especially in volatile markets like penny stocks. While fundamental analysis tells you **what** to buy, technical analysis shows you **when** to buy or sell. Mastering charts, patterns, indicators, and market timing strategies allows investors to make informed decisions, minimize losses, and maximize potential gains.

In this chapter, we will explore the essential tools and techniques used by professional traders to read market signals effectively. You will learn how to identify critical chart patterns such as breakouts, consolidations, and support/resistance levels. We will delve into moving averages (like the 50 EMA and 200 EMA), trend lines, and technical indicators that help predict price momentum and trend reversals.

Additionally, we will cover pre-market and after-hours strategies that can provide early signals before the broader market reacts. To make learning actionable, this chapter includes mini visual examples to enhance pattern recognition and build practical, real-world trading skills.

By the end of this chapter, you will have a systematic framework for using technical analysis to complement your fundamental research, giving you a complete edge in identifying high-potential penny stocks and timing your trades for optimal results.

9.1 Chart Patterns: Breakouts, Consolidation, Support, and Resistance

Chart patterns form the backbone of technical analysis. By understanding how prices behave visually on charts, traders and investors can anticipate potential moves, identify trends, and make more informed entry and exit decisions. Penny stocks, in particular, are highly sensitive to price movements, making pattern recognition an essential skill for anyone seeking multibagger returns.

Breakouts

A **breakout** occurs when the price moves beyond a previously established support or resistance level with increased volume. Breakouts signal that a stock may be entering a new trend, either upward or downward.

- **Bullish Breakout:** When a stock moves above a resistance level, it indicates strong buying pressure and the potential for rapid gains.
- **Bearish Breakout:** A drop below a support level signals strong selling pressure, often leading to further declines.
- **Key Consideration:** Volume is critical. A breakout accompanied by high volume is more likely to sustain than one on low volume, which could be a false signal.
- **Example:** Consider a penny stock trading between $0.80 and $1.00 for several weeks. If it surges to $1.10 with high volume, this breakout may mark the start of a strong upward trend.

Consolidation

Consolidation occurs when a stock trades within a defined range, neither making significant highs nor lows. It reflects market indecision, often preceding a strong price movement.

- **Importance:** Consolidation zones act as accumulation or distribution phases, where investors and traders decide on the next major move.
- **Identifying Patterns:** Rectangles, triangles, and flags often represent consolidation periods. These patterns help predict the breakout direction.
- **Trading Strategy:** Traders often place buy orders near the support of the consolidation zone and sell near resistance, or wait for the breakout to initiate a new trend.

Support and Resistance Levels

Support is a price level where a stock tends to stop falling due to increased buying interest, while **resistance** is a level where upward momentum stalls due to selling pressure.

- **Role in Trading:** Identifying key support and resistance levels helps investors determine entry and exit points, manage risk, and set stop-loss levels.

- **Dynamic Levels:** Moving averages often act as dynamic support or resistance. For example, a 50-day EMA can support a stock in an uptrend, while the 200-day EMA may act as long-term resistance.
- **Psychological Significance:** Round numbers (e.g., $1, $5, $10) often act as psychological support or resistance, especially in penny stocks.
- **Example:** A penny stock repeatedly bouncing off $0.50 indicates strong support. If it breaks below this level, it could trigger panic selling. Conversely, resistance at $1.00 could act as a profit-taking zone until it breaks convincingly.

Integrating Patterns with Volume and Trend Analysis

Chart patterns should never be interpreted in isolation. Combining patterns with volume, trend strength, and other indicators provides higher probability trading signals.

- **Volume Confirmation:** High volume confirms the validity of breakouts or breakdowns.
- **Trend Alignment:** Always align trades with the dominant trend. Trading against strong trends increases risk, especially in low-liquidity penny stocks.
- **Multi-Timeframe Analysis:** Analyzing charts across daily, weekly, and intraday timeframes helps confirm patterns and reduces false signals.

Practical Tips for Penny Stock Traders

1. Keep a trading journal of patterns observed and results.
2. Focus on liquid penny stocks to reduce slippage and false breakouts.
3. Combine pattern recognition with fundamental insights to avoid chasing hype.
4. Use stop-loss orders based on support/resistance levels to manage risk effectively.

By mastering breakouts, consolidation patterns, and support/resistance levels, traders gain a powerful toolkit to navigate the volatile world of penny stocks. Understanding these patterns not only enhances timing decisions but also builds confidence in executing trades, ultimately increasing the probability of identifying high-potential multibagger opportunities.

9.2 Moving Averages, Trend Lines, and Indicators

In the fast-paced world of penny stocks, price action can be volatile and unpredictable. Traders rely on technical analysis tools to make sense of this volatility. Among the most powerful tools are **moving averages**, **trend lines**, and **technical indicators**. These tools help identify trends, support and resistance levels, market momentum, and potential reversals, enabling informed trading decisions.

1. Moving Averages (MA)

A moving average smooths price data over a specific period, allowing traders to see the underlying trend without being distracted by daily fluctuations.

- **Simple Moving Average (SMA):** Calculates the arithmetic mean of prices over a defined period (e.g., 50-day SMA). Useful for identifying long-term trend directions.
- **Exponential Moving Average (EMA):** Gives greater weight to recent prices, making it more responsive to recent market changes. Common periods include 20 EMA (short-term), 50 EMA (medium-term), and 200 EMA (long-term).
- **Applications:**
  - **Trend Direction:** Price above MA indicates an uptrend, below MA signals a downtrend.
  - **Crossovers:** Golden cross occurs when short-term MA crosses above a long-term MA, signaling bullish momentum. Death cross occurs when it crosses below, signaling bearish momentum.
  - **Dynamic Support and Resistance:** MAs often act as natural support or resistance levels where price may bounce or reverse.

2. Trend Lines

Trend lines connect successive highs or lows to visually display the direction of the market. They are essential for spotting trends, reversals, and potential breakout points.

- **Uptrend Line:** Connects ascending lows; indicates support during rising markets.
- **Downtrend Line:** Connects descending highs; acts as resistance in falling markets.
- **Practical Usage:**

- Entry points can be timed along the trend line during pullbacks.
- Breaks above or below trend lines often signal trend reversals.
- Trend lines combined with volume analysis confirm the strength of a breakout.

3. Technical Indicators

Indicators provide quantitative insights into market behavior, supplementing price and trend analysis.

- **Relative Strength Index (RSI):** Measures overbought (above 70) and oversold (below 30) conditions, indicating potential reversal zones.
- **Moving Average Convergence Divergence (MACD):** Tracks the difference between two EMAs to signal momentum shifts or trend changes.
- **Bollinger Bands:** Comprise a moving average and upper/lower bands based on standard deviations, highlighting volatility and potential breakout points.
- **Volume Indicators:** Volume validates price movements; rising volume with rising price signals strength, while rising price with falling volume may indicate a weak trend.

4. Combining Moving Averages, Trend Lines, and Indicators

No single tool is sufficient on its own. High-probability trades emerge when multiple tools align:

- Use MAs to determine primary trend direction.
- Validate breakout or breakdown points with trend lines and volume confirmation.
- Confirm overbought/oversold or momentum conditions with RSI or MACD.
- Multi-timeframe analysis improves reliability by aligning short-term signals with long-term trends.

5. Practical Tips for Penny Stock Traders

1. Focus on liquid penny stocks to reduce false signals caused by erratic price swings.
2. Combine multiple indicators and trend tools rather than relying on a single metric.

3. Adjust settings according to volatility; penny stocks often move faster than large-cap stocks.

4. Maintain a trading journal to record indicator performance, trade outcomes, and patterns for continuous improvement.

Mastering moving averages, trend lines, and technical indicators equips traders with a structured approach to reading price action effectively. This knowledge forms the foundation for identifying entry and exit points, managing risk, and navigating the unpredictable yet potentially rewarding penny stock market.

9.3 Pre-Market and After-Hours Strategies

While most trading occurs during regular market hours, pre-market and after-hours sessions provide unique opportunities—and risks—for penny stock traders. These extended trading sessions allow investors to react to news, earnings reports, and global market movements before the official open or after the official close. Understanding these sessions is crucial for identifying early opportunities, planning entries and exits, and managing risk effectively.

1. What Are Pre-Market and After-Hours Sessions?

- **Pre-Market Trading:** Occurs before the official market open, typically from 4:00 a.m. to 9:30 a.m. EST for U.S. markets. Pre-market trading reflects overnight news, earnings reports, and macroeconomic events.

- **After-Hours Trading:** Takes place after the market closes, generally from 4:00 p.m. to 8:00 p.m. EST in the U.S. These sessions allow traders to respond to earnings releases, corporate announcements, or geopolitical events that occur after regular hours.

- **Global Perspective:** Markets in India, Europe, and Asia have their own pre-market and post-market timings. Traders involved in global penny stocks must adjust to these schedules to capture early signals.

2. Advantages of Trading Outside Regular Hours

- **React Quickly to News:** Earnings announcements, mergers, acquisitions, or macroeconomic data can move stock prices dramatically before the regular session.

- **Identify Early Momentum:** Price spikes or drops in pre-market can signal potential trends for the trading day.

- **Lower Competition:** Fewer traders participate in these sessions, which can provide opportunities for proactive traders to act before the broader market.

3. Risks and Considerations

- **Lower Liquidity:** Pre-market and after-hours trading often has limited volume, which can result in wider bid-ask spreads and higher price volatility.
- **Higher Volatility:** Penny stocks are already volatile; low-volume sessions can magnify price swings, increasing both potential profits and risks.
- **Delayed or Unreliable Data:** Some platforms may have delayed quotes or limited order types, making rapid decision-making more challenging.
- **Market Gaps:** Overnight news can cause opening price gaps that differ significantly from after-hours levels, creating potential slippage.

4. Strategies for Pre-Market Trading

1. **Monitor Key News Sources:** Track earnings releases, press announcements, and economic indicators that affect the stock.
2. **Use Limit Orders:** Avoid market orders in low-liquidity sessions to prevent executing trades at unfavorable prices.
3. **Volume Confirmation:** Ensure pre-market moves are backed by increasing volume to validate momentum.
4. **Set Realistic Targets:** Expect smaller moves compared to regular sessions, and adjust stop-loss levels to account for higher volatility.

5. Strategies for After-Hours Trading

1. **React to Earnings Reports:** Use after-hours sessions to take advantage of earnings surprises or guidance announcements.
2. **Monitor International Markets:** Global economic events and foreign market performance can influence U.S. penny stocks after-hours.
3. **Plan Ahead:** Use after-hours data to formulate strategies for the next regular trading session.
4. **Use Technical Tools Carefully:** Indicators and chart patterns may behave differently in low-volume conditions; combine with fundamentals for validation.

6. Best Practices and Risk Management

- Limit trade size in extended sessions due to lower liquidity.
- Avoid chasing volatile penny stocks immediately after news releases.
- Always have pre-defined entry and exit points, and adjust stops for wider price swings.
- Keep a trading journal to track outcomes of pre-market and after-hours trades for continuous improvement.

By understanding the mechanics of pre-market and after-hours trading, penny stock traders can gain an edge in capturing early price movements, planning more informed trades, and managing risk effectively. While these sessions offer opportunities for profit, they require discipline, preparation, and careful analysis to navigate the heightened volatility and lower liquidity characteristic of extended trading hours.

9.4 Visual Mastery for Pattern Recognition

Recognizing price patterns is one of the most critical skills in technical analysis, especially for volatile penny stocks. Patterns are essentially recurring formations in price movements that reflect underlying market psychology. Mastering visual recognition allows traders to anticipate potential moves, identify high-probability entries and exits, and manage risk more effectively. This section provides a structured, visual approach to learning patterns, combining theory with actionable mini-chart examples.

1. Understanding Core Chart Patterns

Before diving into visuals, it is important to understand the key patterns that traders watch for:

- **Head and Shoulders:** A classic reversal pattern signaling a potential change in trend direction. It consists of three peaks—the left shoulder, the higher head, and the right shoulder. Breakouts below the neckline often confirm a trend reversal.
- **Double Top and Double Bottom:** These patterns signal trend exhaustion. A double top may indicate an impending bearish reversal, whereas a double bottom suggests a bullish reversal.
- **Triangles (Ascending, Descending, Symmetrical):** Triangles represent consolidation before a breakout. The breakout direction often continues the prevailing trend.
- **Flags and Pennants:** Short-term continuation patterns that appear after sharp moves, signaling potential resumption of the trend.

2. Visual Techniques and Mini Charts

Mini charts and simplified visual representations help traders internalize patterns quickly. By breaking down complex movements into smaller, annotated charts, you can develop faster recognition skills:

- **Annotated Mini-Charts:** Highlight key points such as peaks, troughs, support, and resistance zones.
- **Stepwise Pattern Development:** Illustrate how patterns form over time, for example showing each stage of a head and shoulders formation.
- **Color-Coding and Visual Cues:** Use different colors for trendlines, breakout zones, and consolidation areas for immediate visual clarity.
- **Sequential Mini Snapshots:** Break large moves into a series of small charts demonstrating consolidation, breakout, and trend continuation.
- **Contextual Annotations:** Include actionable notes such as potential entry points, stop-loss suggestions, and volume confirmation markers.

3. Practical Tips for Visual Learning

1. **Repetition:** Regular exposure to real charts helps reinforce recognition of patterns under different market conditions.
2. **Annotations:** Mark support, resistance, breakouts, and pullbacks to strengthen visual memory.
3. **Volume Confirmation:** Validate patterns by checking accompanying volume changes—high-volume breakouts are more reliable.
4. **Multiple Timeframes:** Use intraday mini-patterns alongside daily or weekly charts for a complete picture and precise trade timing.
5. **Simulation Practice:** Apply visual recognition on paper trading platforms to reinforce learning without risking capital.

4. Application to Penny Stocks

Penny stocks tend to be highly volatile and can exhibit exaggerated price swings. Developing strong visual pattern recognition is particularly valuable:

- Early detection of breakouts using triangles, flags, and pennants can lead to timely short-term trades.
- Reversal patterns like head and shoulders or double tops/bottoms help avoid losses and capture trend changes.
- Mini visual techniques support quick decision-making when volatility is high and opportunities emerge rapidly.

By combining these visual mastery techniques with consistent practice, pattern recognition becomes intuitive. Traders can anticipate moves, optimize entry and exit points, and improve overall success rates in the challenging penny stock market.

Key Takeaways

- **Chart Patterns Guide Decisions:** Recognizing breakouts, consolidation, support, and resistance levels allows traders to anticipate price movements and plan entries and exits effectively.
- **Moving Averages Provide Trend Clarity:** Indicators such as 50 EMA and 200 EMA help identify the prevailing trend, potential reversals, and dynamic support/resistance levels.
- **Trend Lines Are Essential Tools:** Drawing trend lines allows visualization of price direction, momentum, and breakout/breakdown points.
- **Indicators Confirm Patterns:** Combining chart patterns with technical indicators (RSI, MACD, volume) increases confidence in trading signals and reduces false entries.
- **Pre-Market and After-Hours Strategies Matter:** Understanding trading outside regular hours can reveal early momentum, potential reversals, and unexpected volatility.
- **Visual Techniques Improve Pattern Recognition:** Mini charts, annotations, and color-coded cues accelerate learning and help traders quickly identify actionable setups.
- **Practice Strengthens Mastery:** Repeated analysis of real charts, simulations, and paper trading reinforces pattern recognition, indicator interpretation, and timing accuracy.
- **Integrated Approach:** The combination of chart patterns, moving averages, trend lines, and pre/post-market observation forms a holistic technical analysis framework for better trading decisions.

Chapter 10

Tools, Screeners, and Filters

In the fast-paced world of penny stocks, identifying high-potential opportunities before they move requires more than intuition—it demands the right tools, systematic analysis, and disciplined filtering. This chapter dives into the most effective digital resources and methodologies traders use to screen stocks, filter for quality, and spot early opportunities, while emphasizing caution and risk management.

Penny stocks are notorious for volatility and sudden price spikes. While no tool can guarantee profits, the correct use of stock screeners and filters can significantly increase your probability of identifying promising candidates. Modern platforms provide an unprecedented level of data transparency, from financial metrics to real-time market movements, allowing traders to make informed decisions quickly.

We will explore popular tools and screeners such as **Screener.in, Finviz, Moneycontrol, and TradingView**, showing how each can help analyze fundamentals, technical patterns, and sector-specific trends. Beyond just listing tools, this chapter will guide you on creating custom filters—based on price, volume, debt levels, promoter holdings, and sector potential—to narrow down your watchlist efficiently.

By the end of this chapter, you will not only know which platforms are most suitable for penny stock research but also how to systematically leverage these tools to develop a repeatable and disciplined screening process. This is your foundation for moving from reactive trading to proactive identification of multibagger opportunities, while keeping risk and capital preservation at the forefront.

10.1 Popular Tools and Screeners for Penny Stocks

In the modern trading ecosystem, having access to reliable and comprehensive tools is critical for finding high-potential penny stocks. While no tool guarantees success, the proper use of screeners and analysis platforms can dramatically improve your decision-making and help identify opportunities early. Here, we explore four widely used platforms, each with unique features suited for global traders.

1. Screener.in

Screener.in is a robust tool primarily focused on the Indian stock market. It provides detailed financial statements, key ratios, and customizable filters. Traders can screen for low-priced stocks with strong fundamentals, such as high return on equity, low debt, or growing earnings. The platform also allows users to create watchlists and alerts for stocks meeting specific criteria, making it easier to monitor potential multibaggers in real time. While its primary strength is in India, the concepts of fundamental screening—debt levels, promoter holdings, revenue growth—are universally applicable.

2. Finviz

Finviz is a versatile screener popular among U.S. and global investors. It offers both fundamental and technical screening tools, heatmaps, and charting capabilities. Users can filter stocks based on market capitalization, price, volume, sector, and financial metrics. For penny stock traders, Finviz's ability to visualize data quickly through heatmaps and sortable tables helps in spotting unusual activity, such as sudden volume spikes or undervalued small-cap stocks. Its global stock coverage allows traders to compare opportunities across multiple markets.

3. Moneycontrol

Moneycontrol is an India-centric platform offering news, financial data, analysis, and market updates. It provides an easy interface for screening small-cap and penny stocks, tracking daily movements, and monitoring sector trends. Beyond fundamental data, Moneycontrol delivers timely news alerts, earnings reports, and promoter activity insights, which are critical for understanding risk in penny stocks. Global traders can learn from its methodologies and replicate similar strategies using local platforms in their markets.

4. TradingView

TradingView is a global platform renowned for its advanced charting capabilities, custom indicators, and social network of traders. Unlike other screeners,

TradingView emphasizes technical analysis, enabling traders to overlay multiple indicators, draw trendlines, and test strategies using historical data. Its ability to scan global exchanges and integrate real-time news makes it a valuable tool for identifying intraday and swing opportunities. Traders can also share scripts and trading strategies within the community, accelerating learning and refining pattern recognition skills.

Key Considerations Across Platforms

- **Accessibility:** Some platforms are free, others require subscriptions; global users should evaluate cost versus functionality.
- **Data Accuracy:** Always cross-check financial data and market prices, especially in volatile penny stocks.
- **Customization:** Build filters and alerts that match your investment strategy rather than relying on default settings.
- **Global Relevance:** Understand your local exchange rules, trading hours, and tax implications; not all tools provide full coverage outside their primary market.

By integrating these platforms into a structured workflow, traders can combine fundamental insights, technical analysis, and real-time alerts to create a disciplined approach to identifying high-potential penny stocks across different markets.

10.2 Identifying Penny Stocks Before Price Spikes

One of the most sought-after skills for penny stock traders is the ability to spot stocks before they experience significant price movements. Early identification can potentially lead to substantial returns, but it is critical to emphasize that penny stocks are inherently volatile, and there are no guarantees of profit. A disciplined, research-driven approach combined with reliable tools can improve your probability of success while managing risk effectively.

Understanding Price Spikes

Price spikes occur when a stock experiences a rapid increase in price over a short period. In penny stocks, these movements are often exaggerated due to low liquidity and small market capitalization. Common drivers include:

- **Positive news or announcements:** Earnings beats, new contracts, or regulatory approvals can trigger sudden interest.

- **Market sentiment shifts:** Social media trends, analyst recommendations, or sectoral momentum can influence traders.
- **Low float and volume:** Stocks with limited shares available for trading can react sharply to even modest buying pressure.

Tools and Techniques for Early Identification

While there is no foolproof method to predict spikes, traders can leverage screeners and monitoring tools to increase their awareness of potential movers:

- **Volume Analysis:** Watch for unusual spikes in trading volume, which often precede price movements.
- **Price Breakouts:** Track stocks approaching historical resistance or key technical levels for potential breakout opportunities.
- **Fundamental Catalysts:** Monitor news feeds and financial releases to anticipate sudden interest in undervalued stocks.
- **Real-Time Alerts:** Configure screener alerts for unusual activity in price, volume, or volatility to respond quickly.

Cautionary Guidelines

Because penny stocks are prone to manipulation and extreme swings, it is crucial to combine identification methods with strict risk management:

- **No Guarantees:** Even well-researched stocks can underperform or drop suddenly; always prepare for losses.
- **Avoid Herd Mentality:** Be skeptical of social media hype, "pump and dump" schemes, and unverified tips.
- **Limit Capital Exposure:** Never commit more than a small portion of your portfolio to highly speculative trades.
- **Paper Trading:** Test spike-identification strategies in simulation before committing real capital.

Integrating with a Trading Strategy

Identifying potential spikes should not be a standalone activity. Combine it with:

- Fundamental analysis to ensure the stock has long-term potential.
- Technical analysis to confirm breakout patterns or support/resistance levels.

- A clearly defined exit strategy, including stop-loss and profit-taking rules.

By approaching penny stock spikes systematically—leveraging volume, price patterns, news catalysts, and alerts—traders can enhance their ability to react quickly, while keeping risk under control. Discipline and preparation, rather than guesswork or speculation, separate consistent performers from casual traders in the volatile world of penny stocks.

10.3 Filtering Penny Stocks by Key Metrics

Identifying high-potential penny stocks requires more than luck or random scanning. Systematic filtering using objective criteria allows traders and investors to narrow down thousands of options into a manageable, high-probability set of candidates. While no filter guarantees success, combining multiple metrics improves the likelihood of discovering multibagger opportunities while controlling risk.

1. Filtering by Price

Price is the most obvious starting point for penny stock screening. Typically, stocks under a defined threshold—such as $5 in the U.S. or INR 10–20 in India—are considered penny stocks. However, price alone does not indicate value. Key considerations include:

- **Absolute Price vs. Relative Value:** A low-priced stock may still be overvalued relative to earnings or book value.
- **Volatility Awareness:** Penny stocks fluctuate more dramatically, so even small price changes can represent significant percentage gains or losses.
- **Liquidity Considerations:** Extremely low-priced stocks may have low trading volume, making entry and exit challenging.

2. Filtering by Volume

Trading volume is a critical indicator of market interest and liquidity:

- **Average Daily Volume:** Identify stocks with consistent trading activity to reduce the risk of price manipulation.
- **Volume Spikes:** Sudden surges may indicate increased attention or an upcoming breakout, but verify the reason behind the spike.
- **Volume vs. Float:** Stocks with a small float and high volume are more volatile and require careful risk management.

3. Filtering by Debt-Free Status

Financial health is vital even for small-cap and penny stocks:

- **Debt-to-Equity Ratio:** Prefer stocks with minimal debt to reduce bankruptcy or solvency risk.
- **Interest Coverage:** Ensure the company can comfortably service its interest obligations, even during market downturns.
- **Balance Sheet Strength:** Look for positive net assets, adequate cash reserves, and manageable liabilities.

4. Filtering by Sectors

Sector selection helps align investments with macro trends and growth potential:

- **High-Growth Sectors:** Technology, renewable energy, electric vehicles, biotech, and defense often produce multibagger opportunities.
- **Cyclical vs. Defensive:** Understand sector-specific risks and volatility; cyclical sectors may spike faster but can also decline sharply.
- **Diversification:** Avoid concentrating all penny stock picks in one sector to reduce sector-specific risk.

5. Filtering by Promoter Holdings

Promoter ownership reflects confidence and potential alignment with minority shareholders:

- **High Promoter Holdings:** Can indicate long-term commitment to company growth.
- **Insider Transactions:** Frequent selling by promoters may signal financial stress or lack of confidence.
- **Regulatory Disclosures:** Track mandatory filings to understand insider behavior and potential red flags.

Integrating Filters for a Systematic Approach

Effective screening combines multiple metrics:

1. Start with price and volume to ensure the stock is tradable and liquid.
2. Check financial health via debt ratios, net assets, and profitability indicators.

3. Evaluate sector tailwinds and macro trends for growth potential.
4. Assess promoter holdings and insider activity to gauge management commitment.

By systematically applying these filters, traders and investors can reduce noise, focus on higher-probability opportunities, and build a disciplined approach to penny stock investing. Remember, no screening method guarantees success—risk management, diversification, and continuous learning are essential for navigating volatile markets effectively.

Key Takeaways

- Effective penny stock research requires using reliable screening tools such as Screener.in, Finviz, Moneycontrol, and TradingView.
- Identifying potential stock movements before spikes can provide an edge, but no tool guarantees success—always approach with caution.
- Filtering by key metrics improves selection:
  - **Price:** Focus on low-priced stocks but assess value relative to fundamentals.
  - **Volume:** Ensure sufficient liquidity for easier entry and exit.
  - **Debt-Free Status:** Prioritize financially healthy companies with manageable liabilities.
  - **Sectors:** Align stock picks with high-growth or trending sectors to maximize upside potential.
  - **Promoter Holdings:** High promoter ownership indicates confidence and long-term commitment.
- Combining multiple filters systematically increases the probability of finding high-potential penny stocks.
- Continuous learning, validation, and risk management are essential; screens only provide candidates, not guaranteed winners.

Chapter 11

Market Sentiment & News

In the fast-moving world of penny stocks, market sentiment and timely information can make or break a trade. While fundamentals and technical analysis provide a framework for selecting high-potential stocks, staying informed about news, corporate announcements, earnings reports, and overall market sentiment is equally crucial.

Penny stocks are particularly sensitive to perception. A single news release, regulatory update, or social media post can trigger sharp price movements. Understanding how to interpret information, separate noise from actionable data, and recognize market psychology is essential for reducing risk and improving trading outcomes.

In this chapter, we explore how to track reliable news sources, responsibly leverage social media platforms like Reddit, Twitter, and Telegram, and avoid common pitfalls such as hype, pump-and-dump schemes, and misinformation. By mastering market sentiment, traders and investors can make more informed decisions, anticipate potential moves, and identify opportunities that others might overlook.

11.1 Tracking News, Earnings Reports, and Official Announcements

Staying informed is a cornerstone of successful penny stock trading. Unlike large-cap stocks, penny stocks are extremely sensitive to information, and even small updates can trigger significant price swings. This section explores how to systematically track news, earnings, and official announcements to gain an edge while minimizing risk.

1. News Sources and Their Importance

Reliable news sources are essential for understanding market sentiment and potential catalysts. Traders should consider:

- **Financial News Portals:** Websites like Bloomberg, Reuters, Economic Times, Moneycontrol, and MarketWatch provide verified corporate updates, economic data, and sectoral news.
- **Exchange Announcements:** Official stock exchange notifications (e.g., NSE, BSE, Nasdaq, NYSE) contain filings, corporate actions, and regulatory updates. These are authoritative sources and often precede market reactions.
- **Press Releases:** Direct corporate announcements can include product launches, partnerships, management changes, or fundraising events that may influence stock prices.
- **Investor Relations Pages:** Many companies maintain dedicated IR sections on their websites where quarterly reports, presentations, and investor communications are published.

2. Earnings Reports and Financial Updates

Earnings reports are critical indicators of a company's financial health and growth potential:

- **Quarterly and Annual Reports:** Analyze revenue growth, profit margins, debt levels, and cash flow. Consistent improvement often signals potential multibagger candidates.
- **Earnings Surprises:** Unexpected results—either positive or negative—can trigger rapid price movements. Monitoring earnings calendars ensures you are aware of these key dates.
- **Forward Guidance:** Companies' future outlook statements often impact investor sentiment more than past performance. Positive guidance may indicate expansion plans or new opportunities.

3. Official Announcements and Regulatory Filings

Regulatory compliance and official filings provide transparency and reduce uncertainty:

- **Corporate Actions:** Stock splits, dividends, buybacks, mergers, and acquisitions can significantly influence penny stock behavior.
- **Insider Transactions:** Buying or selling by promoters and executives can indicate confidence or concern. These filings are typically public and can be tracked systematically.
- **Delisting Notices:** Penny stocks are often at higher risk of delisting. Monitoring official exchange announcements helps avoid being trapped in illiquid, de-listed stocks.

4. Best Practices for Tracking Information

1. **Set Up Alerts:** Use apps, email notifications, and financial platforms to get real-time updates on stocks of interest.
2. **Maintain a News Log:** Record important news, announcements, and earnings data to correlate with past price movements.
3. **Cross-Verify Information:** Avoid acting on unverified rumors; always confirm data with official sources or multiple credible outlets.
4. **Integrate With Analysis:** Combine news insights with fundamental and technical analysis to make informed decisions rather than reactive trades.

By actively tracking verified news, earnings reports, and official announcements, traders gain actionable insights that improve timing, identify catalysts, and enhance the probability of success in the volatile penny stock market. Consistency and discipline in following this approach are key to turning information into actionable strategy.

11.2 Using Social Media Responsibly: Reddit, Twitter, Telegram

In today's fast-paced financial markets, social media has emerged as a double-edged sword for traders. Platforms such as Reddit, Twitter, and Telegram provide real-time news, market sentiment insights, and crowd-driven trends. While these platforms can offer early signals about penny stocks and emerging opportunities, they are also rife with misinformation, hype, and manipulative schemes. Understanding how to use these tools responsibly is crucial for making informed, rational trading decisions.

1. The Power and Pitfalls of Social Media in Trading

Social media accelerates the flow of information, often outpacing traditional news outlets. For penny stocks, which are highly volatile and less liquid, social media can heavily influence price movements in a short period.

- **Reddit:** Communities like `r/WallStreetBets`, `r/IndianStockMarket`, and other regional forums discuss penny stocks, share analysis, and sometimes rumors. Participating in these communities requires discernment, as posts are often unverified.
- **Twitter:** Known for instant updates, Twitter hosts analysts, journalists, and investors sharing opinions, news, and insights. Hashtags and trending topics can highlight shifts in market sentiment.

- **Telegram:** Provides fast, real-time alerts through channels focused on specific stocks or sectors. While speed is an advantage, unregulated groups are prone to hype, unverified tips, and even coordinated manipulation.

2. Common Risks of Social Media for Penny Stock Traders

Penny stocks' low market capitalization makes them highly susceptible to price manipulation. Social media can amplify both opportunities and risks.

- **Pump-and-Dump Schemes:** Coordinated campaigns artificially inflate a stock's price before the promoters exit, leaving unsuspecting traders with losses.
- **Misinformation and Rumors:** Unverified tips, fake news, or anecdotal claims can cause impulsive trades.
- **Emotional Trading:** Social media can trigger fear of missing out (FOMO) or panic selling, leading to poor risk management.
- **Herd Mentality:** Following the crowd without analysis increases the probability of losses.

3. Best Practices for Responsible Social Media Use

1. **Verify Information:** Cross-check any tip or news with credible sources such as official exchange filings, company announcements, or verified financial news portals.
2. **Follow Credible Accounts and Communities:** Focus on analysts or groups with a proven track record rather than anonymous, sensationalist accounts.
3. **Limit Exposure:** Avoid being glued to feeds and notifications, which can lead to impulsive decisions.
4. **Use Social Media as a Supplement:** Combine insights from social media with fundamental and technical analysis rather than relying solely on online chatter.
5. **Document and Analyze:** Maintain a log of observed patterns, verified news, and actionable insights to build a personal knowledge base over time.

4. Integrating Social Media Insights Into Your Trading Strategy

When used responsibly, social media can significantly enhance market awareness and decision-making:

- **Trend Spotting:** Early identification of sector rotations or market-moving news.
- **Sentiment Confirmation:** Use online discussions to gauge the mood of retail investors, confirming or questioning your analysis.
- **Opportunity Identification:** Spot potential trades faster, but always cross-verify with fundamentals and technical indicators.

5. Key Takeaways

- Social media is a tool, not a trading strategy; use it to supplement, not replace, analysis.
- Penny stocks are highly susceptible to hype; exercise caution with any online-driven signals.
- Verification, discipline, and documentation are the cornerstones of responsible social media trading.

By integrating verified social media insights with fundamental and technical analysis, traders can enhance their decision-making and improve the probability of success in volatile penny stock markets.

11.3 Avoid Hype, Pump-and-Dump Schemes, and Misinformation

Penny stocks are particularly vulnerable to manipulation due to their low liquidity, small market capitalization, and limited public information. One of the most critical skills for any trader or investor is the ability to distinguish genuine market opportunities from hype, scams, and misinformation. Understanding these risks and learning how to navigate them can protect your capital and improve long-term outcomes.

1. Understanding Market Hype

Hype occurs when excitement around a stock grows disproportionately compared to its underlying fundamentals. It can originate from social media posts, newsletters, chat groups, or even news outlets. Hype often creates a temporary surge in stock price, luring inexperienced traders into impulsive decisions.

- **Signs of Hype:** Rapid price spikes without corresponding news, excessive social media chatter, and sensational headlines.
- **Impact on Traders:** Hype can trigger FOMO (fear of missing out), causing emotional rather than rational trading decisions.

- **Mitigation:** Always cross-check claims against official filings, financial statements, and reliable news sources.

2. Pump-and-Dump Schemes

Pump-and-dump is a classic form of stock manipulation, often associated with penny stocks. Here's how it typically works:

1. **Pump Phase:** Manipulators promote a stock aggressively via emails, social media, chat groups, or newsletters. The goal is to attract uninformed investors, inflating the stock price.
2. **Dump Phase:** Once the price is artificially high, manipulators sell their holdings, leaving new investors holding devalued shares.

Key Lessons:

- High volatility, unusually high trading volume, and aggressive promotion are red flags.
- Verify trading activity and news with credible sources before making decisions.
- Be cautious of anonymous tips and "guaranteed" gains—it's almost always too good to be true.

3. Misinformation and Fake News

Misinformation can spread quickly, especially on social media platforms. False reports, misleading headlines, or fabricated insider information can distort market perception. Penny stocks are particularly susceptible because they have lower analyst coverage and limited financial transparency.

- **Examples:** Fake press releases, false regulatory announcements, or exaggerated claims about new contracts or products.
- **Consequences:** Traders acting on misinformation may face significant losses when the truth emerges.
- **Prevention:** Always cross-verify information from multiple credible sources, and rely on official filings, company announcements, and reputable financial news platforms.

4. Practical Tips to Avoid Pitfalls

1. **Focus on Fundamentals:** Prioritize companies with transparent financials, sustainable business models, and credible management teams.
2. **Analyze Volume and Price Behavior:** Look for abnormal spikes that aren't backed by news or fundamentals.

3. **Limit Social Media Influence:** Use online chatter as a secondary input, not the primary reason for buying or selling.
4. **Maintain a Trading Journal:** Document decisions, sources of information, and lessons learned to avoid repeating mistakes.
5. **Set Risk Controls:** Always use stop-losses and define the maximum amount of capital to risk per trade.

5. Key Takeaways

- Hype, pump-and-dump schemes, and misinformation are pervasive in penny stock markets.
- Recognize red flags such as rapid price surges, aggressive promotion, and anonymous tips.
- Always verify information through multiple credible sources before taking action.
- Focus on fundamentals, disciplined risk management, and evidence-based strategies.
- Developing skepticism and critical analysis is essential for long-term trading success.

By maintaining a disciplined approach, combining verification with analysis, and staying emotionally detached from hype, traders can navigate the volatile penny stock landscape more safely and improve the probability of consistent success.

Chapter Key Takeaways

- **Track Official Sources:** Always prioritize earnings reports, press releases, regulatory filings, and company announcements over unofficial news. Verified sources provide the most reliable insights for decision-making.
- **Use Social Media Responsibly:** Platforms like Reddit, Twitter, and Telegram can offer market sentiment and early signals, but they are often unverified. Treat social media chatter as supplementary information, not as the primary basis for trades.
- **Recognize Hype:** Rapid price surges, excessive chatter, and sensational headlines often indicate market hype. Avoid making impulsive decisions based on emotion or FOMO (Fear of Missing Out).

- **Avoid Pump-and-Dump Schemes:** Be cautious of stocks being aggressively promoted online. Understand that manipulators may artificially inflate prices to sell their holdings at a profit, leaving new investors with losses.
- **Validate Information:** Cross-check all news and tips using multiple credible sources. Misinformation spreads quickly, especially for low-cap penny stocks with minimal analyst coverage.
- **Focus on Fundamentals:** Even when monitoring sentiment and news, your trading decisions should prioritize company fundamentals, financial health, and credible growth potential.
- **Risk Management is Key:** Set stop-losses, define capital allocation, and maintain disciplined trade execution to mitigate losses in volatile markets.
- **Develop Critical Thinking:** Cultivate skepticism and analytical skills to differentiate genuine opportunities from hype, scams, or misinformation. This skill is essential for long-term success in penny stock trading.

By combining verified market news, responsible social media monitoring, and disciplined risk management, traders can make more informed decisions and navigate the volatile penny stock environment safely.

Part IV

Strategies for Multibagger Success

Chapter 12

Shortlisting High-Potential Penny Stocks

Identifying potential multibagger penny stocks is both an art and a science. Success in this realm requires a careful combination of fundamental analysis, technical evaluation, and market intuition. While penny stocks are inherently risky, a structured approach can help you separate genuine opportunities from fleeting hype.

This chapter guides you through the process of early identification of high-potential penny stocks by:

- **Combining Fundamentals and Technicals:** Learn how to assess the financial health, growth potential, and sector positioning of a company while using technical signals to time entry and exit points effectively.
- **Historical Case Studies:** Explore real-life examples of penny stocks that have delivered 10x, 20x, or even 50x returns. Understand what set them apart, and what patterns and strategies contributed to their explosive growth.
- **Practical Mini-Checklist:** Develop a repeatable screening process for spotting multibagger candidates, including key financial metrics, price behavior, and early market signals.

By the end of this chapter, you will have a systematic framework for evaluating penny stocks and prioritizing those with genuine potential for extraordinary growth, while minimizing avoidable risks. This structured approach lays the foundation for disciplined, repeatable, and informed investment decisions in the highly volatile penny stock market.

12.1 Combining Fundamentals and Technicals for Early Identification

Investing in penny stocks is not simply about spotting the lowest-priced shares or following market hype. True multibagger potential lies in a disciplined approach that integrates both **fundamental analysis** and **technical analysis**. By combining these methods, investors can identify stocks with solid intrinsic value that are also showing early signs of upward price momentum, allowing for well-timed entries and higher probability trades.

1. Fundamental Analysis: Understanding the Company's Core

Fundamental analysis is the backbone of identifying penny stocks with sustainable growth potential. Key areas to focus on include:

- **Financial Health:** Evaluate balance sheets, income statements, and cash flow statements. Look for companies with low debt, consistent revenue growth, and improving profit margins. Strong fundamentals indicate the company can withstand market volatility.
- **Promoter and Insider Holdings:** High promoter ownership often signals confidence in the company's future. Insider buying or selling can provide additional clues about management's belief in growth prospects.
- **Sector and Industry Tailwinds:** Industries experiencing rapid growth, such as AI, EVs, renewable energy, healthcare, or defence, provide a fertile ground for high returns. A penny stock in a booming sector is more likely to attract investor attention.
- **Competitive Advantage:** Assess whether the company has unique products, technologies, patents, or operational efficiencies that differentiate it from competitors. A competitive moat increases the likelihood of long-term success.
- **Valuation Metrics:** Use ratios like Price-to-Book (P/B), Price-to-Earnings (P/E), and debt-to-equity to gauge whether a stock is undervalued relative to its peers.

2. Technical Analysis: Timing and Market Behavior

While fundamentals reveal *what* to buy, technical analysis answers *when* to buy. Key techniques include:

- **Trend Identification:** Use moving averages, trendlines, and momentum indicators to spot early upward or downward trends.

- **Support and Resistance Levels:** Recognize price points where the stock historically finds buying support or faces selling pressure. These levels guide entry and exit decisions.
- **Volume Analysis:** Rising trading volumes during breakouts confirm genuine market interest, while unusually low volumes can indicate manipulation or illiquidity.
- **Pattern Recognition:** Identify classic chart patterns such as breakouts, triangles, flags, or head-and-shoulders formations, which often precede significant price moves.
- **Momentum Indicators:** Tools like RSI (Relative Strength Index), MACD (Moving Average Convergence Divergence), and stochastic oscillators help detect overbought or oversold conditions.

3. Integrating Fundamentals and Technicals

The power of this approach lies in integration. Here's a step-by-step methodology:

1. **Screen with Fundamentals First:** Filter penny stocks with strong financials, low debt, promising growth, and sector tailwinds.
2. **Apply Technical Filters:** Analyze charts for trends, breakout patterns, and confirmed support/resistance zones.
3. **Validate with Market Sentiment:** Cross-check news, earnings reports, and social sentiment to avoid overhyped stocks or pump-and-dump traps.
4. **Rank Candidates:** Assign scores based on financial strength and technical signals to prioritize high-probability multibagger opportunities.

4. Benefits of a Combined Approach

- **Higher Probability Trades:** Focus on fundamentally strong companies showing early technical momentum.
- **Risk Mitigation:** Avoid purely speculative trades by ensuring solid intrinsic value.
- **Systematic Investing:** Develop a repeatable process that reduces emotional decision-making and reliance on luck.
- **Early Advantage:** Spotting trends before the broader market increases the potential for outsized returns.

By consistently applying a combined fundamentals and technicals approach, investors can systematically uncover penny stocks with genuine growth potential. This methodology transforms trading from a speculative gamble into a disciplined, data-driven process, maximizing the likelihood of capturing multibagger returns while minimizing avoidable risks.

12.2 Historical Case Studies: 10x, 20x, 50x Returns

The most powerful way to understand penny stocks is through real-world examples. By studying historical multibagger case studies, investors gain insights into the factors that can drive extraordinary returns, the risks involved, and the strategies that separate winners from losers. This section explores notable cases from India, the United States, and global markets, emphasizing lessons applicable today.

1. Indian Penny Stock Success Stories

India has seen remarkable success stories in small-cap and penny stock investing. These examples show how a combination of innovation, timing, and disciplined investment can produce outsized returns:

- **Company A (Illustrative Example):** Bought at INR 5, sold at INR 250 in five years a 50x return. Strong management, entry into high-growth sectors like renewable energy, and steady financial growth drove the performance.
- **Company B:** From INR 20 to INR 400 in four years 20x return. Growth was fueled by sector tailwinds, expanding market share, and solid fundamentals.
- **Company C:** From INR 10 to INR 100 in three years 10x return. Strategic partnerships and market recognition played key roles.

Lesson: Early identification, robust fundamentals, and sectoral tailwinds are critical factors for multibagger potential.

2. U.S. Penny Stock Phenomena

The U.S. markets, especially OTC and small-cap Nasdaq stocks, have a history of producing dramatic returns. Investors who combine patience with technical and fundamental analysis can capture remarkable gains:

- **Stock X:** \$0.50 → \$25 in five years (50x). Technology sector adoption and consistent revenue growth were primary drivers.

- **Stock Y:** \$2 → \$40 in four years (20x). Strategic acquisitions and insider confidence fueled the rise.
- **Stock Z:** \$1 → \$10 in two years (10x). Benefited from market recognition, strong earnings growth, and momentum.

Lesson: High-growth sectors combined with technical momentum can create multibagger opportunities, but timing is essential.

3. Common Themes Across Markets

Examining multibaggers across geographies highlights common patterns:

- **Early Identification:** Recognizing strong fundamentals before market hype is key.
- **Patience and Discipline:** Holding through volatility enables compounding.
- **Sector Tailwinds:** Rapidly growing industries often produce the largest gains.
- **Quality Management:** Aligned promoters and competent leadership increase success probability.
- **Technical Timing:** Combining fundamental research with chart patterns improves entry and exit decisions.

4. Lessons from Failures

Not all promising penny stocks succeed. Common reasons for failure include:

- Regulatory challenges or forced delistings.
- Management missteps or fraudulent activities.
- Market hype without supporting fundamentals.
- Liquidity issues preventing timely exits.

Lesson: Learning from failures is as important as studying winners. Risk management, due diligence, and diversification are critical.

5. Applying Historical Insights Today

Investors can use historical cases as benchmarks:

1. Compare valuation, growth, and risk profiles with historical multibaggers.

2. Analyze the timing and market conditions that produced rapid gains.
3. Combine lessons from multiple markets to identify global opportunities.
4. Avoid blindly following trends; focus on fundamentals, sector growth, and technical validation.

Conclusion: Historical multibagger case studies show that exceptional returns are rare but achievable with disciplined analysis, strategic entry, and an understanding of sector trends. By internalizing these lessons, investors can enhance their probability of discovering the next high-potential penny stock.

12.3 Mini-Checklist for Identifying Multibagger Candidates

Identifying potential multibagger penny stocks requires a disciplined approach. While no checklist guarantees success, using a structured framework can significantly improve the probability of selecting high-potential candidates. This section provides a comprehensive mini-checklist covering key criteria that investors should consider before committing capital.

1. Fundamental Health

- **Revenue Growth:** Look for companies with consistent year-over-year revenue growth, ideally above industry averages.
- **Profitability Metrics:** Positive net income, improving profit margins, and manageable debt indicate financial stability.
- **Balance Sheet Strength:** Low debt-to-equity ratios, sufficient cash reserves, and healthy working capital are critical.
- **Promoter Holdings:** High promoter or insider stake often signals alignment with shareholder interests.
- **Earnings Quality:** Prefer companies with recurring revenue streams over one-time windfalls.

2. Market Position and Sector Dynamics

- **Sector Growth Potential:** Focus on industries poised for expansion—AI, EV, renewable energy, pharma, and emerging technologies.
- **Competitive Advantage:** Unique products, patents, or strategic partnerships strengthen multibagger potential.
- **Market Share:** Increasing or stable market share indicates a strong positioning relative to peers.

3. Valuation Metrics

- **Price-to-Earnings (P/E) Ratio:** Compare with industry peers; undervalued stocks with growth potential may outperform.
- **Price-to-Book (P/B) Ratio:** Low P/B relative to fundamentals can indicate hidden value.
- **Debt Levels:** Companies with manageable debt can withstand market volatility better.

4. Technical Indicators

- **Trend Analysis:** Check whether the stock is in a clear uptrend or consolidation phase ready for breakout.
- **Volume Patterns:** Rising volume during upward price movements confirms market interest.
- **Support and Resistance Levels:** Identify entry points near strong support zones and plan exits at resistance points.

5. Risk Assessment

- **Liquidity:** Ensure sufficient trading volume to enter and exit positions without significant slippage.
- **Regulatory and Compliance Risk:** Check for delisting risks, pending litigations, or regulatory scrutiny.
- **Volatility Management:** Be aware of historical price swings and prepare stop-loss or scaling strategies.

6. Market Sentiment and News

- **News Analysis:** Monitor earnings reports, corporate announcements, and sector developments.
- **Social Signals:** Use Reddit, Twitter, and financial forums for sentiment, but avoid hype-driven decisions.
- **Expert Opinions:** Compare analyst ratings and research notes for corroborating signals.

7. Actionable Summary

By systematically applying this checklist, investors can:

1. Filter out high-risk candidates without strong fundamentals.

2. Identify penny stocks with multibagger potential early.
3. Combine fundamental and technical insights to improve timing.
4. Manage risks while maintaining exposure to high-reward opportunities.

Conclusion: While no framework can guarantee a multibagger, a disciplined approach using this mini-checklist allows investors to systematically evaluate potential candidates, improving their odds of achieving outsized returns in the volatile world of penny stocks.

Key Takeaways

- **Buy-and-Hold Approach:** Long-term investment in fundamentally strong penny stocks can yield multibagger returns if patience and discipline are maintained.
- **Momentum Trading:** Short-term trading based on market trends and price action can provide additional gains, but requires active monitoring and quick decision-making.
- **Gradual Scaling:** Incrementally increasing positions allows you to manage risk while capitalizing on potential upside.
- **Diversified Allocation:** Never allocate all capital to one stock; spread investments across multiple high-potential candidates to reduce risk.
- **Strategy Combination:** Blending long-term and short-term strategies can balance risk and reward, enhancing overall portfolio performance.
- **Risk Awareness:** Consistently evaluate market conditions, volatility, and liquidity to protect capital and optimize returns.

Chapter 13

Investment & Trading Strategies

Investing in penny stocks requires more than luck—it demands a clear strategy, discipline, and an understanding of both short-term market movements and long-term potential. This chapter explores actionable approaches that can help you navigate the volatile world of small-cap and penny stocks while maximizing your potential for multibagger returns.

Why Strategy Matters

Penny stocks are inherently high-risk and high-reward. Without a well-defined strategy, investors can easily fall prey to market volatility, hype, or impulsive decisions. A structured investment plan helps manage risk, optimize entry and exit points, and systematically grow wealth over time.

Overview of Key Approaches

- **Buy-and-Hold for Long-Term Multibaggers:** Focusing on fundamentally strong penny stocks and holding them over extended periods can compound gains, turning small investments into life-changing returns.

- **Short-Term Momentum Trading:** For traders comfortable with active participation, capitalizing on short-term price movements can offer significant gains. This requires technical analysis, market awareness, and disciplined execution.

- **Gradual Scaling:** Incrementally building positions allows you to manage exposure while benefiting from upward trends. This approach reduces risk compared to investing all capital at once.

- **Allocation Strategies:** Diversifying investments across multiple stocks and sectors helps mitigate losses, protects capital, and creates a balanced portfolio that can capture growth from various opportunities.

How This Chapter Helps You

By the end of this chapter, you will understand how to combine long-term and short-term strategies, plan entry and exit points, and allocate capital intelligently. You will gain practical frameworks for turning high-risk opportunities into calculated, repeatable, and potentially life-changing investments.
Whether you are a beginner seeking structure or an active trader looking for tactical guidance, these strategies provide the foundation for disciplined, profitable, and sustainable penny stock investing.

13.1 Buy-and-Hold for Long-Term Multibaggers

Investing in penny stocks with a long-term perspective can unlock exponential growth potential. Unlike short-term trading, which relies heavily on timing and market sentiment, a buy-and-hold approach focuses on identifying fundamentally strong companies and holding them over extended periods, allowing time and compounding to work in your favor.

Why Buy-and-Hold Works

- **Compounding Over Time:** The longer a high-quality penny stock is held, the more opportunity it has to multiply, as reinvested earnings and market recognition drive price growth.
- **Reduced Emotional Interference:** Long-term holding minimizes impulsive decisions influenced by fear, greed, or short-term market fluctuations.
- **Fundamental Focus:** By emphasizing company health, revenue growth, management quality, and sector potential, investors avoid speculative traps and focus on genuine value creation.
- **Capturing Multibagger Potential:** Many penny stocks require years to realize their full potential. Patience allows investors to fully benefit from market trends and industry tailwinds.

Steps to Implement Buy-and-Hold

1. **Screen for Strong Fundamentals:** Look for companies with robust balance sheets, low debt, growing revenue, strong cash flows, and competent management teams.

2. **Evaluate Industry and Sector Trends:** Choose sectors with long-term growth prospects, such as technology, renewable energy, healthcare, and emerging industries.

3. **Define Goals and Timeframe:** Set clear return expectations and holding periods. Multibagger opportunities often require 3–7 years or more to fully materialize.

4. **Monitor Strategically:** Regularly review earnings reports, company announcements, and sector developments, but avoid overreacting to minor market fluctuations.

5. **Diversify Within Penny Stocks:** Reduce risk by holding a portfolio of 5–10 carefully researched penny stocks.

Real-World Examples

- **Tech Startup Example:** Purchased at $0.50, grew to $25 in five years due to strong fundamentals and sector growth.
- **Renewable Energy Example:** Early investment of $1 reached $40 in six years, driven by government incentives and growing sector demand.
- **Emerging Market Success:** A small-cap healthcare company grew from $2 to $60 over seven years, exemplifying the power of long-term investment in a promising sector.

Best Practices for Long-Term Success

- Avoid following hype or unverified tips; rely on thorough research.
- Stay focused on long-term trends rather than short-term market noise.
- Reinvest dividends to accelerate compounding returns.
- Maintain patience and discipline—this mindset often separates ordinary investors from those achieving multibagger wealth.

By adhering to a disciplined buy-and-hold strategy, investors can leverage time, fundamentals, and market growth to transform modest penny stock investments into significant multibagger returns.

13.2 Short-Term Momentum Trading and Gradual Scaling

While buy-and-hold focuses on long-term growth, short-term momentum trading allows traders to capitalize on price movements within days, weeks, or months. This strategy is particularly effective in penny stocks, where volatility is higher and sudden price surges can generate substantial gains. When combined with gradual scaling, traders can manage risk while optimizing returns.

Understanding Momentum Trading

- **Definition:** Momentum trading involves buying stocks that are moving strongly in one direction—up or down—on significant volume and selling before the trend reverses.
- **Core Principle:** "The trend is your friend." Traders aim to ride price movements rather than predict reversals.
- **Time Horizon:** Positions can be held from a few hours to several weeks, depending on the stock's volatility and market conditions.
- **Indicators Used:** Common indicators include Relative Strength Index (RSI), Moving Averages, MACD, and volume spikes.

Gradual Scaling Approach

- **Incremental Entry:** Instead of investing the entire capital at once, break your allocation into smaller portions and buy as momentum confirms strength.
- **Partial Profit Booking:** Take profits in stages as the stock moves in your favor, ensuring gains are realized while keeping a position for further upside.
- **Stop-Loss Adjustments:** Use trailing stop-loss orders to protect gains as the stock moves up. Gradually tighten stop-loss levels as momentum matures.
- **Reinvestment Strategy:** Allocate profits from successful trades into new momentum opportunities to compound gains over time.

Key Steps for Momentum Trading

1. **Identify High-Volume Movers:** Scan for penny stocks with sudden price spikes and increased trading volume.
2. **Analyze Technical Signals:** Confirm trend strength using charts, support/resistance levels, and technical indicators.
3. **Determine Entry Point:** Buy on pullbacks within the upward trend to reduce risk and optimize entry price.
4. **Set Targets and Stops:** Define realistic profit targets and stop-loss levels before entering the trade.

5. **Scale Gradually:** Add to winning positions or reduce exposure in losing trades to manage risk effectively.

Advantages and Risks

- **Advantages:** Quick profits, flexibility, ability to capitalize on volatile penny stock moves.
- **Risks:** High volatility can lead to rapid losses, sudden reversals, and emotional decision-making.
- **Mitigation:** Use strict risk management, position sizing, and gradual scaling techniques to limit exposure.

Real-World Application

- A penny stock surges 20% in a day due to positive news. By entering incrementally and setting a trailing stop, a trader can secure partial gains while still participating in further upside.
- Gradual scaling allows multiple trades in a single stock without risking full capital at one price point.
- Combining momentum trading with fundamental analysis ensures that trades are grounded in some underlying value rather than pure speculation.

By mastering short-term momentum trading and gradual scaling, traders can take advantage of penny stock volatility while maintaining disciplined risk control, allowing for both capital preservation and consistent gains over time.

13.3 Allocation Strategies to Minimize Risk

Successful trading and investing in penny stocks requires more than just identifying potential winners—it demands careful capital allocation to protect against volatility and unexpected losses. Proper allocation strategies balance risk and reward, ensuring that a portfolio can survive downturns while capturing growth opportunities.

Principles of Risk-Based Allocation

- **Diversification:** Spread investments across multiple stocks, sectors, or market segments to avoid overexposure to a single position.
- **Position Sizing:** Determine the maximum percentage of capital to allocate to any one stock, typically ranging between 1%–5% for high-risk penny stocks.

- **Risk-Reward Ratio:** Allocate more capital to trades with favorable risk-reward setups. Assess potential gains versus potential losses before committing.
- **Volatility Consideration:** High-volatility stocks should have smaller allocations compared to more stable investments to reduce portfolio swings.

Gradual and Tiered Allocation

- **Staggered Entry:** Enter positions in tranches rather than all at once. This allows adjustment based on market movement and reduces the risk of buying at a peak.
- **Scaling Into Winners:** Increase allocation to stocks that show consistent upward momentum while maintaining a cap to avoid concentration risk.
- **Partial Exits:** Take profits incrementally. This preserves capital while locking in gains and freeing funds for new opportunities.

Portfolio Construction Techniques

- **Core-Satellite Approach:** Maintain a core portfolio of stable, low-risk assets (large-caps, ETFs) while allocating a smaller "satellite" portion to high-risk, high-reward penny stocks.
- **Sector Diversification:** Spread exposure across sectors such as technology, energy, healthcare, and finance to reduce sector-specific shocks.
- **Correlation Analysis:** Choose stocks with low correlation to each other to smooth overall portfolio volatility.

Dynamic Allocation and Rebalancing

- **Regular Review:** Periodically assess performance of positions and overall portfolio risk exposure.
- **Rebalancing:** Adjust allocations to maintain desired risk levels. Trim positions that have grown disproportionately or increase positions in underweighted areas with strong potential.
- **Capital Rotation:** Move funds from matured or overbought stocks into new opportunities with better risk-reward potential.

Risk Management Tools

- **Stop-Loss Orders:** Automatic triggers to exit positions when a predefined loss threshold is reached.
- **Trailing Stops:** Lock in gains while allowing for upside participation.
- **Hedging Strategies:** Use options or inverse ETFs (where available) to reduce downside risk.
- **Cash Reserve:** Maintain liquidity to capitalize on sudden opportunities and to buffer against portfolio drawdowns.

Practical Example

Suppose a trader has $10,000 to invest in penny stocks:

- Allocate 70% ($7,000) to diversified core investments and blue-chip stocks.
- Allocate 30% ($3,000) to penny stocks, split across 6–8 different high-potential names.
- Enter each penny stock in two tranches, with 50% of the allocation initially and the remaining 50% as the stock confirms upward momentum.
- Apply stop-losses and take partial profits to lock in gains while leaving room for upside.

By following systematic allocation strategies, traders can participate in high-risk, high-reward opportunities while minimizing the likelihood of catastrophic losses. Discipline, ongoing monitoring, and a structured approach are key to sustainable success in penny stock investing.

Key Takeaways

- **Buy-and-Hold for Long-Term Multibaggers:** Patience is critical. Holding high-potential penny stocks over the long term allows compounding and increases the likelihood of achieving multibagger returns.
- **Short-Term Momentum Trading:** Capitalize on intraday or swing movements by tracking market trends, volume spikes, and technical indicators. Always combine momentum strategies with strict risk management.
- **Gradual Scaling:** Avoid investing all capital at once. Enter positions in tranches and scale into winning trades to minimize risk and optimize returns.

- **Allocation Strategies:** Diversify across multiple stocks and sectors. Limit exposure to high-volatility penny stocks and maintain a core-satellite portfolio structure for stability.
- **Position Sizing and Risk Management:** Determine how much capital to allocate per trade based on risk-reward ratios, volatility, and correlation. Use stop-losses, trailing stops, and partial exits to protect capital.
- **Regular Portfolio Rebalancing:** Review and adjust allocations periodically. Trim positions that have grown disproportionately and rotate capital into emerging opportunities to maintain balanced risk exposure.
- **Combine Fundamentals and Technicals:** Long-term multibagger potential is best identified through a mix of financial health analysis and technical chart patterns.
- **Discipline and Consistency:** Successful trading relies on sticking to defined strategies, maintaining emotional control, and avoiding impulsive decisions based on hype or fear.
- **Documentation and Learning:** Track trades, outcomes, and lessons learned. Continuous learning and adapting based on experience improves decision-making over time.

Chapter 14

Risk Management & Safety Nets

In the world of penny stocks and high-potential small-cap investments, the potential for huge gains comes hand-in-hand with significant risks. Without a robust risk management framework, even the most promising opportunities can quickly lead to devastating losses. This chapter focuses on building a strong foundation to protect your capital, manage emotional and market risks, and ensure sustainable growth in your portfolio.
We will explore key principles that every investor must adopt:

- **Diversification:** Avoid putting all your capital into a single stock. Spread your investments across multiple stocks, sectors, and asset classes to minimize risk exposure.
- **Stop-Loss Strategies and Exit Plans:** Define clear exit points for each trade and stick to them. Using stop-loss orders and pre-planned exit strategies prevents emotional decision-making during market volatility.
- **Emotional Risk Management:** Fear, greed, and FOMO (Fear of Missing Out) are powerful forces that can derail even disciplined investors. Learn to recognize and control these emotions to make objective, rational trading decisions.
- **Avoiding Scams, Manipulation, and Over-Leverage:** Penny stocks are often targets of pump-and-dump schemes and other manipulations. Maintaining vigilance and avoiding excessive leverage is critical to preserving your capital and sanity.

By the end of this chapter, you will have a clear understanding of how to create your own safety nets, implement actionable risk management strategies, and trade with confidence, even in highly volatile markets. This framework is not just about avoiding losses—it is about building a foundation that allows your investments to grow sustainably and consistently over time.

14.1 Diversification: Never Put All Your Capital in One Stock

One of the cardinal rules of investing, especially in the volatile world of penny stocks, is diversification. Concentrating your entire capital in a single stock may offer the allure of enormous gains, but it exponentially increases the risk of catastrophic loss. Diversification spreads your investment across multiple securities, sectors, and even asset classes, reducing the impact of a single adverse event.

Why Diversification Matters

- **Mitigates Volatility:** Penny stocks are notorious for wild price swings. By spreading investments across several stocks, a loss in one position may be offset by gains in another, stabilizing overall portfolio performance.

- **Protects Against Company-Specific Risks:** Even fundamentally strong companies can face unexpected challenges—regulatory issues, management missteps, or market downturns. Diversification ensures that a single negative event does not wipe out your entire portfolio.

- **Capitalizes on Multiple Opportunities:** By investing in multiple high-potential penny stocks, you increase the probability of hitting a multibagger while balancing the inherent risks.

Diversification Strategies

1. **Across Stocks:** Spread your investments among at least 5–10 different penny stocks, ideally in various industries or sectors.

2. **Across Sectors:** Diversify between technology, healthcare, renewable energy, consumer goods, and other sectors to reduce sector-specific risk.

3. **Across Geographies:** If possible, include stocks from different markets—domestic and international—to hedge against country-specific economic or regulatory shocks.

4. **Across Asset Classes:** Complement penny stock holdings with mid-cap, large-cap, bonds, ETFs, or even commodities to further reduce overall portfolio risk.

Practical Examples

Consider an investor with $10,000 to allocate:

- $1,000 each in 5 high-potential penny stocks across different sectors.
- $2,000 in a mid-cap index ETF.
- $2,000 in a large-cap blue-chip company with stable dividends.

In this scenario, even if one penny stock fails completely, the overall portfolio can still perform well due to gains or stability in other holdings.

Tips for Effective Diversification

- Avoid over-diversifying; too many small positions can dilute gains and make monitoring difficult.
- Regularly review and rebalance the portfolio based on performance, sector trends, and emerging opportunities.
- Use position sizing to allocate more to higher-conviction ideas while keeping overall risk controlled.

Key Principle: Diversification is not just a defensive tactic—it is a strategic approach that enables growth while managing risk. It allows you to pursue high returns from penny stocks without exposing your entire capital to unnecessary peril.

14.2 Stop-Loss Strategies and Exit Plans

In the volatile world of penny stocks, mastering risk control is just as important as selecting high-potential opportunities. Stop-loss strategies and well-defined exit plans act as your safety nets, protecting capital and ensuring that losses remain manageable. Without them, even a single unexpected market movement can erode months or years of gains.

What is a Stop-Loss?

A stop-loss is a pre-set order to sell a stock automatically when its price reaches a specific level. This mechanism helps prevent emotional decision-making and limits downside risk.

- **Protects Capital:** By defining the maximum tolerable loss upfront, stop-loss orders prevent catastrophic damage to your portfolio.
- **Removes Emotional Bias:** Fear and greed can cloud judgment. Automated stop-loss orders ensure discipline, even in highly volatile markets.

- **Supports Strategy Execution:** Stop-losses allow you to follow your trading strategy systematically rather than reacting impulsively.

Types of Stop-Loss Orders

1. **Fixed Stop-Loss:** Sell the stock if it drops to a predetermined price. Simple and widely used.
2. **Trailing Stop-Loss:** The stop price moves up as the stock price rises, locking in gains while still allowing upside potential.
3. **Percentage-Based Stop-Loss:** Set the stop-loss at a fixed percentage below your entry price (e.g., 10%). This standardizes risk across positions.
4. **Volatility-Based Stop-Loss:** Adjust the stop-loss according to the stock's historical volatility, allowing more room for naturally fluctuating stocks while still protecting against sharp declines.

Designing Effective Exit Plans

A robust exit plan is about knowing when to take profits, cut losses, and reallocate capital:

- **Profit Targets:** Determine levels at which you will sell part or all of your position. This prevents greed from eroding gains.
- **Scaling Out:** Gradually sell portions of your holdings as the stock rises, securing profits while leaving room for further upside.
- **Time-Based Exits:** If a stock fails to perform within a set time frame, consider exiting to free capital for better opportunities.
- **Event-Driven Exits:** Major news, earnings, or regulatory changes may trigger exits even if the stock hasn't hit predefined stop-loss or profit targets.

Practical Examples

Example 1: Fixed Stop-Loss You buy a penny stock at $1.00 and set a stop-loss at $0.85 (15% loss). The stock drops to $0.85, triggering an automatic sale. Loss is limited and prevents emotional decisions.
Example 2: Trailing Stop-Loss Purchase price: $1.00. Stock rises to $1.50. Trailing stop of 10% moves the stop to $1.35, protecting gains if the stock falls sharply from its peak.

Tips for Effective Stop-Loss and Exit Planning

- Always set stop-losses at the time of purchase—never retroactively.
- Avoid placing stop-losses too tight, which could trigger unnecessary exits due to normal volatility.
- Combine stop-losses with technical analysis for more precise levels based on support, resistance, and chart patterns.
- Review and adjust exit plans regularly based on performance and market conditions.

Key Principle: Stop-loss strategies and exit plans are not a sign of weakness—they are essential tools that protect your capital, enhance decision-making, and enable consistent growth in the high-risk world of penny stocks.

14.3 Emotional Risk Management: Fear, Greed, and FOMO

In the high-volatility world of penny stocks, mastering your emotions can be the difference between consistent profits and catastrophic losses. Emotional biases—fear, greed, and the Fear of Missing Out (FOMO)—can sabotage even the most well-planned investment strategies. This section explores these emotions, their impact on trading decisions, and practical techniques to manage them effectively.

Understanding Fear in Trading

Fear often manifests when the market moves against your position or when uncertainty looms over a particular stock or sector. While fear can protect from unnecessary risk, excessive fear can prevent you from seizing opportunities.

- **Paralysis by Analysis:** Overthinking every decision can lead to missed trades.
- **Selling Prematurely:** Fear may trigger early exits, preventing participation in potential multibagger gains.
- **Over-Protection:** Over-reliance on stop-losses without proper positioning may result in consistently small gains.

Strategies to Manage Fear:

- Set predefined entry and exit points to reduce uncertainty.
- Practice paper trading to build confidence in decision-making.
- Focus on probability-based thinking rather than gut reactions.

Greed: The Double-Edged Sword

Greed can push traders to take excessive risks, over-leverage positions, or ignore warning signals. While ambition is necessary, unchecked greed can lead to losses that far exceed potential gains.

- **Overtrading:** Chasing every spike in penny stocks can drain capital quickly.
- **Ignoring Fundamentals:** Greed may blind traders to poor financial metrics or high risk.
- **Emotional Scaling:** Failing to scale out of positions at appropriate profit targets.

Strategies to Manage Greed:

- Define realistic profit targets and stick to them.
- Use scaling strategies to secure partial profits while keeping exposure to upside.
- Maintain a disciplined portfolio allocation to prevent overexposure to a single stock.

FOMO (Fear of Missing Out)

FOMO often drives impulsive buying during hype cycles or social media-driven frenzies. This emotional response can lead to entering positions at inflated prices, chasing short-term momentum rather than long-term strategy.

- **Social Pressure:** Posts, news, and forums may make traders feel "left out."
- **Chasing Hype:** Jumping into spikes without due diligence often results in losses.
- **Timing Errors:** FOMO can cause late entries, increasing downside risk.

Strategies to Combat FOMO:

- Stick to a pre-defined watchlist and entry criteria.
- Focus on research-backed trades rather than trending stocks.
- Maintain a trading journal to evaluate past decisions and learn from FOMO-driven mistakes.

Building Emotional Discipline

The key to emotional risk management is consistent discipline. Techniques include:

- **Meditation and Mindfulness:** Helps reduce impulsive reactions to market volatility.
- **Journaling:** Documenting trades, emotions, and outcomes to identify patterns.
- **Routine Review:** Weekly or monthly review of trades to separate decisions driven by data from those driven by emotion.
- **Peer Accountability:** Discussing trades with mentors or trading communities to mitigate biased decisions.

Practical Example

Imagine a penny stock surges 50% in one day due to viral social media attention. A trader succumbing to FOMO might enter at the peak, only to face a sharp reversal. In contrast, a disciplined trader with defined entry criteria, stop-losses, and a clear risk-reward plan can avoid emotional traps and protect capital.
Key Takeaway: Emotional mastery is as important as technical skill in penny stock trading. By recognizing and managing fear, greed, and FOMO, traders can make rational, consistent, and profitable decisions even in highly volatile markets.

14.4 Avoiding Scams, Market Manipulation, and Over-Leverage

Trading penny stocks is highly rewarding but inherently risky. Beyond natural market volatility, investors face additional threats: scams, market manipulation, and over-leveraging. Understanding these dangers and implementing preventive strategies is crucial to protect capital and maintain consistent growth.

Understanding Scams in Penny Stocks

Penny stocks, often thinly traded and lightly regulated, are prime targets for fraudulent schemes. Common scams include:

- **Pump-and-Dump:** Fraudsters artificially inflate a stock's price through misleading statements, then sell at the peak, leaving late investors with losses.

- **Insider Trading:** Promoters or insiders exploit non-public information to trade profitably at the expense of ordinary investors.
- **Fake Promotions and News:** Misleading newsletters, blogs, or social media posts that exaggerate a stock's potential.

Prevention Strategies:

- Always verify company filings, official announcements, and financial statements.
- Avoid investing based solely on online hype, rumors, or unsolicited tips.
- Prefer stocks listed on regulated exchanges with transparency and reporting requirements.

Recognizing Market Manipulation

Market manipulation can occur in various forms:

- **Wash Trading:** Repeated buying and selling to create artificial volume.
- **Churning:** Brokers or insiders excessively trade positions to generate commissions or alter prices.
- **Spoofing:** Placing large buy/sell orders without intention to execute, to influence perception.

Protective Measures:

- Track unusual volume spikes or price movements without fundamental justification.
- Compare multiple data sources to validate trends.
- Maintain a cautious position size in volatile stocks.

Over-Leverage: A Silent Killer

Using borrowed funds or excessive margin can amplify profits—but also losses. Over-leverage is especially dangerous in penny stocks due to high volatility and liquidity constraints.

- **Margin Risks:** Sudden price drops can trigger margin calls, forcing liquidation at a loss.
- **Psychological Pressure:** Leveraged positions increase stress, often leading to impulsive decisions.

- **Portfolio Vulnerability:** One misstep can wipe out multiple positions if not managed carefully.

Mitigation Techniques:

- Limit leverage to conservative levels; avoid "all-in" positions.
- Diversify capital across multiple stocks and sectors.
- Use stop-loss orders and predefined exit strategies to cap potential losses.

Red Flags to Watch For

- Promises of guaranteed returns or "secret" strategies.
- Sudden spikes in social media chatter or newsletters pushing a stock.
- Companies with inconsistent or opaque financial statements.
- Excessive insider selling or unusual promoter activity.

Best Practices for Safe Trading

- Conduct thorough due diligence before every investment.
- Maintain a trading journal to document decisions, mistakes, and lessons.
- Focus on risk-adjusted returns rather than chasing the next 10x opportunity.
- Regularly review regulatory updates and exchange notices.

Key Takeaway

Scams, market manipulation, and over-leverage are major pitfalls in penny stock trading. Awareness, disciplined risk management, and adherence to verified information sources are essential to protect capital and build sustainable wealth. Treat every trade as a calculated decision, not a gamble, and always prioritize safety over speculation.

Key Takeaways

- **Diversification:** Spread capital across multiple stocks and sectors to reduce the impact of a single loss. Never put all your funds into one investment.
- **Stop-Loss and Exit Plans:** Define clear stop-loss levels and exit strategies before entering a trade to protect against sudden market reversals.

- **Emotional Risk Management:** Control emotions like fear, greed, and FOMO. Decisions should be guided by analysis and strategy, not impulsive reactions.

- **Awareness of Scams and Manipulation:** Penny stocks are vulnerable to fraud, pump-and-dump schemes, and market manipulation. Stay informed, verify information, and rely on credible sources.

- **Avoid Over-Leverage:** Using excessive borrowed funds magnifies both gains and losses. Keep leverage conservative to maintain sustainable trading and protect capital.

- **Discipline and Preparedness:** Treat every trade as a calculated decision. Combine careful planning, systematic risk management, and vigilance to navigate volatile markets successfully.

Chapter 15

Real-Life Case Studies

Understanding theory is important, but real-world examples breathe life into the concepts. In this chapter, we dive into actual journeys of investors, traders, and companies that illustrate the high-risk, high-reward nature of penny stocks. By analyzing both extraordinary successes and cautionary failures, readers can extract practical lessons and avoid common pitfalls. We explore:

- **Jordan Belfort and Stratton Oakmont:** Classic lessons on market psychology, hype, and the consequences of unethical practices, with clear disclaimers highlighting legal and ethical considerations.
- **Indian Multibagger Penny Stock Journeys:** Inspiring examples from the Indian markets where disciplined research, patience, and calculated risk-taking led to exponential returns.
- **Lessons from Winners and Losers:** An actionable synthesis of key takeaways from both triumphs and failures, helping readers build a practical playbook for their own investing strategy.

By combining historical insights, ethical considerations, and real trading experiences, this chapter equips readers with a deeper understanding of how penny stocks can create life-changing wealth and the traps to avoid along the way.

15.1 Jordan Belfort & Stratton Oakmont

Jordan Belfort, famously known as the "Wolf of Wall Street," and his brokerage, Stratton Oakmont, offer some of the most dramatic examples of both the potential and the perils of aggressive trading in penny stocks. While his story has been widely publicized in books and films, it is crucial to separate the entertainment from actionable lessons, and to understand the legal and ethical boundaries that Belfort repeatedly crossed.

1. The Allure of High Returns

Stratton Oakmont thrived by selling speculative and often illiquid stocks to uninformed investors, generating enormous commissions. This highlights the magnetic appeal of penny stocks:

- **Explosive Potential:** Small-cap and low-priced stocks can yield massive percentage gains in a short time.
- **Market Psychology:** Investor fear and greed can dramatically amplify price movements, creating rapid short-term opportunities.

2. The Dangers of Manipulation

Despite the allure, Stratton Oakmont's methods were illegal, involving market manipulation and misrepresentation. Key warnings include:

- **Pump-and-Dump Risks:** Artificially inflating stock prices before selling can lead to catastrophic losses for retail investors.
- **Legal Consequences:** Engaging in unethical practices can result in fines, imprisonment, and permanent damage to your reputation.

3. Lessons on Sales and Persuasion

One neutral takeaway from Belfort's story is the extraordinary sales techniques used:

- **Confidence and Clarity:** Persuasive communication, structured pitches, and clear explanations are essential skills in finance.
- **Ethical Application:** Learn from the techniques, but apply them responsibly to educate and provide value rather than mislead.

4. Risk Awareness and Emotional Discipline

The Stratton Oakmont saga underscores the dangers of unchecked greed:

- **Emotional Control:** Avoid chasing quick gains without proper analysis or risk management.
- **Systematic Approach:** High returns are rarely sustainable without a structured, disciplined approach.

5. Takeaways for Penny Stock Investors

From Belfort's rise and fall, we can distill several actionable lessons:

- Prioritize research, due diligence, and ethical investing over hype.
- Use sales and persuasion skills to understand markets and investors, not to manipulate them.
- Always implement risk management: stop-losses, diversification, and realistic position sizing.
- Treat extreme volatility with respect; never over-leverage.
- Understand that short-term gains are tempting, but long-term sustainable strategies build real wealth.

Disclaimer: This section is intended for educational purposes only. The strategies used by Belfort and Stratton Oakmont involved illegal and unethical practices. This book does not endorse, encourage, or condone any form of market manipulation or fraud. The lessons extracted focus on psychology, risk awareness, and ethical investing.

15.2 Indian Multibagger Penny Stock Journeys

India's stock market has been fertile ground for multibagger penny stocks small-cap companies that have delivered extraordinary returns over time. Unlike dramatic international stories like Stratton Oakmont, Indian multibagger journeys are grounded in a combination of strong fundamentals, market timing, and sector tailwinds. Studying these examples provides valuable insights into spotting high-potential opportunities and understanding the risks involved.

1. Early Movers in Emerging Sectors

Many Indian multibaggers originated in sectors that were poised for rapid growth, such as technology, pharmaceuticals, renewable energy, and niche industrials.

- **Case Example: A Tech Startup Turned Multibagger**
  In the early 2000s, a small software services company listed at under INR 10 per share. By focusing on global IT outsourcing demand and consistently increasing revenues, it delivered over 50x returns in less than a decade. Key lessons include the importance of sector growth, leadership, and sustainable business models.

- **Case Example: Pharma and Healthcare Innovation**
  Several mid-2000s pharmaceutical firms, initially trading at sub-20 prices, benefited from global demand for generics and strong R&D pipelines. Investors who spotted early earnings growth and solid management were rewarded with 20x–30x returns.

2. Identifying Patterns in Indian Markets

Indian multibaggers often exhibit recurring characteristics:

- **Low Initial Market Cap:** Companies with small capitalization have higher potential for large percentage gains.
- **Strong Promoter Holdings:** Committed promoters with aligned incentives often drive consistent growth.
- **Sector Tailwinds:** Favorable government policies or market trends amplify growth.
- **Transparency and Governance:** Companies adhering to compliance and financial disclosure are more likely to sustain growth.

3. The Role of Timing and Patience

Multibagger returns rarely happen overnight. Key timing considerations include:

- **Market Cycles:** Many penny stocks surge during economic expansions or sector-specific booms.
- **Holding Period:** Long-term patience often separates winners from short-term traders.
- **Capitalizing on Volatility:** Short-term fluctuations can be used to scale into positions, but must be paired with a disciplined approach.

4. Real Lessons from Indian Investors

Several retail investors in India have shared insights from multibagger journeys:

- **Do Your Homework:** Detailed fundamental and technical research is critical before investing.
- **Avoid Herd Mentality:** Early identification often means investing before the stock becomes widely popular.
- **Exit Strategically:** Even multibaggers require periodic assessment; know when to book profits without fear.

- **Risk Management:** Never invest all capital in one small-cap stock; diversification and position sizing protect against unforeseen market shocks.

5. Key Takeaways from Indian Multibagger Journeys

- Multibaggers are more probable in small-cap and emerging sectors with strong fundamentals.
- Patience and disciplined holding amplify returns, even in volatile markets.
- Promoter quality, governance, and sector tailwinds are critical factors for success.
- Combining research, risk management, and timing increases the probability of identifying multibagger candidates.

By studying these Indian penny stock journeys, investors can develop a framework for spotting high-potential opportunities and navigating the risks inherent in volatile small-cap markets. Understanding these patterns and lessons forms the foundation for building a repeatable, long-term wealth creation strategy.

15.3 Lessons from Winners and Losers with Actionable Takeaways

Investing in penny stocks and small-cap companies can produce life-changing returns, but the path is fraught with risks. Studying the experiences of both winners and losers allows investors to extract actionable insights. By analyzing what worked, what failed, and why, you can develop a disciplined, repeatable approach to wealth creation.

1. Lessons from Winners

Successful penny stock investors share common traits and strategies that distinguish them from the average trader:

- **Thorough Research:** Winners conduct both fundamental and technical analysis before committing capital. They evaluate balance sheets, promoter holdings, market position, and industry trends.
- **Early Identification:** Multibaggers are often discovered before they gain widespread attention. Winners spot potential before hype drives prices.

- **Patience and Discipline:** Long-term holding allows compounding to work in favor of the investor. Winners resist the urge to exit prematurely during short-term volatility.
- **Risk Management:** Position sizing, diversification, and pre-set stop-losses protect capital. Even winners accept that losses are part of the journey.
- **Learning from Mistakes:** They analyze failed trades to refine strategies, avoid repeating errors, and improve decision-making.

2. Lessons from Losers

Losses provide equally valuable insights. Common pitfalls include:

- **Chasing Hype:** Following social media or friends' tips without proper analysis often leads to losses.
- **Over-Leverage:** Using excessive margin or investing all capital in a single stock increases vulnerability to sudden market swings.
- **Ignoring Fundamentals:** Buying without considering company financials or sector potential can result in holding failing stocks.
- **Emotional Trading:** Fear, greed, and FOMO (fear of missing out) drive impulsive decisions that erode capital.
- **Poor Exit Strategies:** Waiting too long to cut losses or taking profits too early reduces long-term returns.

3. Actionable Takeaways

By combining lessons from both winners and losers, investors can build a structured framework for penny stock investing:

1. **Do Your Homework:** Always perform due diligence. Analyze fundamentals, technicals, sector growth, and macroeconomic factors.
2. **Diversify Your Portfolio:** Avoid putting all capital into a single stock. Spread risk across multiple potential multibaggers.
3. **Set Entry and Exit Rules:** Predetermine buy and sell points based on analysis and risk tolerance. Stick to these rules to minimize emotional decisions.
4. **Use Position Sizing and Stop-Losses:** Allocate a percentage of capital per trade and enforce stop-losses to limit downside risk.
5. **Leverage Mini Research and Tools:** Utilize screeners, charting tools, and financial news responsibly to identify trends early.

6. **Stay Patient and Avoid Hype:** Wait for the right opportunity. Avoid impulsive trades driven by short-term market noise.
7. **Review and Learn Continuously:** After every trade, analyze the outcome—whether win or loss—to improve future decisions.

4. Real-World Application

Consider this scenario:

- **Stock A:** An emerging tech company with solid earnings and committed promoters. Early research revealed strong growth potential. The investor applied a long-term buy-and-hold strategy, diversified with other penny stocks, and gradually scaled positions. Outcome: 25x return over 5 years.
- **Stock B:** A small-cap stock hyped on social media with no clear fundamentals. The investor bought aggressively, ignored stop-loss rules, and sold during panic selling. Outcome: 80% loss in 6 months.

The contrast highlights the importance of disciplined research, risk management, and emotional control. Winners combine strategy with patience, while losers often fall prey to hype and impulsivity.

5. Summary of Key Principles

- Research trumps speculation.
- Diversification protects capital.
- Emotional discipline is as important as analytical skills.
- Risk management—through position sizing and stop-losses—minimizes catastrophic losses.
- Learning from both success and failure creates a repeatable framework for long-term wealth creation.

By internalizing these lessons, readers can approach penny stock investing with a structured, informed, and disciplined mindset—significantly increasing their chances of identifying true multibagger opportunities while mitigating avoidable risks.

Key Takeaways

- **Learn from Both Successes and Failures:** Analyzing real-world case studies provides invaluable insights into what drives gains and what causes losses in penny stock investing.

- **Ethical Awareness Matters:** Jordan Belfort and Stratton Oakmont illustrate the consequences of unethical practices. Always prioritize legal compliance and ethical trading.
- **Identify Growth Early:** Indian multibagger journeys show that spotting companies with strong fundamentals, committed promoters, and sector tailwinds early can yield extraordinary returns.
- **Combine Fundamentals and Technicals:** Success often comes from analyzing both financials and market behavior, rather than relying solely on tips, hype, or emotions.
- **Risk Management is Crucial:** Winners consistently apply stop-losses, diversification, and position sizing, whereas losers often fail due to over-leverage and emotional trading.
- **Discipline Over Impulse:** Avoid chasing hype, social media trends, or "get-rich-quick" schemes. Consistency, patience, and calculated decisions create long-term wealth.
- **Actionable Lessons are Repeatable:** Takeaways from both successes and failures should form a structured framework that can be applied systematically for future trades.
- **Volatility Presents Opportunity and Risk:** Penny stocks can produce 10x, 20x, or even 50x returns—but without strategy and risk controls, they can also wipe out capital quickly.

Part V

Advanced Growth & Portfolio Mastery

Chapter 16

Sectoral Plays & Future Trends

Investing in penny stocks is not just about picking individual companies—it's about understanding the broader sectors they operate in. Certain industries naturally provide fertile ground for rapid growth, fueled by innovation, policy support, and shifting market demands. In this chapter, we dive into the sectors that have consistently produced multibagger opportunities and explore emerging trends that could define the next generation of wealth creation.
We will examine sectors such as Artificial Intelligence (AI), Electric Vehicles (EV), Pharma, Renewable Energy, Defence, Nuclear, and the rapidly evolving Web3 ecosystem. Each of these areas carries unique growth drivers, risks, and market dynamics that can influence the performance of penny stocks within them.
By combining sector-specific tailwinds with strong company fundamentals, investors can identify high-potential opportunities before they become mainstream. This chapter will provide you with a structured approach to evaluate sectoral trends, align them with your investment strategy, and harness them to uncover multibagger potential.

16.1 High-Growth Sectors: Understanding Opportunities and Drivers

Investing in high-growth sectors is a cornerstone of identifying potential multibagger stocks. While individual companies may rise and fall, certain sectors consistently demonstrate strong tailwinds, structural growth, and innovation-led opportunities. For penny stock investors, understanding these sectors provides context, helps narrow down screening, and increases the probability of selecting early-stage winners. Below we examine seven high-growth sectors, why they matter, and what drives their potential.

1. Artificial Intelligence (AI)

AI is rapidly transforming industries by automating processes, generating insights, and enabling new business models. Companies involved in machine learning, natural language processing, computer vision, and predictive analytics are seeing unprecedented adoption.

Why it matters: AI adoption is growing globally, with governments and corporations investing billions in AI research and infrastructure. Penny stocks in AI-related products or services often have the potential to scale rapidly once their solutions gain traction.

Key drivers: Data availability, cloud computing, algorithmic innovation, and regulatory acceptance.

2. Electric Vehicles (EV)

EVs are at the forefront of the global transition toward sustainable transportation. Beyond car manufacturers, the EV ecosystem includes battery technology, charging infrastructure, and EV software solutions.

Why it matters: EV adoption is supported by government incentives, environmental policies, and consumer demand for cleaner alternatives. Companies positioned early in battery production or EV components can experience exponential growth.

Key drivers: Battery efficiency, vehicle range, infrastructure expansion, and supportive policy frameworks.

3. Pharmaceuticals (Pharma)

Pharma is a sector with both defensive and high-growth characteristics. Startups in biotech, generic drugs, and innovative therapies can deliver massive upside, particularly when linked to successful clinical trials or regulatory approvals.

Why it matters: Healthcare demand is rising globally due to aging populations, increasing chronic diseases, and innovation in treatment. Penny stocks in pharma often act as high-risk, high-reward vehicles.

Key drivers: R&D breakthroughs, patent approvals, regulatory changes, and market adoption.

4. Renewable Energy

Renewable energy companies focus on solar, wind, hydro, and energy storage solutions. Global decarbonization initiatives are driving significant investments in this sector.

Why it matters: As governments and corporations aim for net-zero emissions, renewable energy adoption accelerates. Early-stage companies in solar panels, wind turbines, and energy storage can deliver multibagger potential.

Key drivers: Policy incentives, technological advances, energy demand, and global environmental goals.

5. Defence

Defence companies produce military equipment, cybersecurity solutions, and advanced defense technology. Geopolitical tensions and national security budgets ensure ongoing demand.

Why it matters: Stable government contracts and innovation in defense technology create opportunities for consistent growth. Penny stocks in this sector can surge with new contracts or technological breakthroughs.

Key drivers: Government budgets, export deals, innovation, and global geopolitical shifts.

6. Nuclear Energy

Nuclear energy is gaining renewed attention as a low-carbon power source. Companies involved in nuclear reactors, fuel supply, and technology innovations are at the forefront.

Why it matters: Nuclear offers stable, long-term energy solutions, and companies in this space may benefit from policy shifts toward clean energy. Penny stocks in this sector can see large price movements based on regulatory approvals or contracts.

Key drivers: Energy policies, regulatory approvals, technological advances, and safety innovations.

7. Web3 and Blockchain Technologies

Web3, decentralized finance (DeFi), NFTs, and blockchain platforms represent the digital frontier. Companies building infrastructure, smart contracts, or tokenized assets often have disruptive potential.

Why it matters: Web3 technologies are redefining finance, ownership, and digital interactions. Early-stage penny stocks may benefit from adoption and network effects, though volatility is high.

Key drivers: Technology adoption, regulatory clarity, network effects, and innovative applications.

Conclusion: Sector-Driven Multibagger Potential

Understanding high-growth sectors is essential for any investor seeking multibagger returns. By combining sector tailwinds with strong company fundamentals, early-stage investors can identify opportunities where small investments may compound into significant wealth. These sectors are particularly fertile for penny stocks due to their potential for rapid growth, innovation, and market expansion.

Investors should always balance high-reward potential with risk management, staying informed about sector-specific trends, regulatory changes, and macroeconomic factors that could impact returns.

16.2 Sector Tailwinds + Fundamentals: The Multibagger Formula

Identifying multibagger stocks requires more than luck—it requires a systematic approach combining macro-level sector growth and micro-level company fundamentals. By understanding the interplay between sector tailwinds and a company's financial health, growth potential, and strategic positioning, investors can tilt the odds in their favor.

1. Understanding Sector Tailwinds

Sector tailwinds are the macroeconomic, technological, regulatory, and demographic forces that drive growth in a particular industry. These tailwinds create an environment where companies can scale faster than the broader market.

- **Technology and Innovation:** Sectors like AI, EVs, and Web3 benefit from continuous innovation, creating opportunities for early movers.
- **Regulatory Support:** Government policies, subsidies, and tax incentives can accelerate growth in renewable energy, EVs, and defence.
- **Demographic Shifts:** Aging populations increase demand in healthcare and pharma, while younger tech-savvy consumers drive adoption in digital platforms.
- **Global Trends:** International market expansion, globalization, and digital adoption provide additional growth leverage.

2. Assessing Company Fundamentals

While sector tailwinds provide the backdrop, company-specific fundamentals determine whether a firm can capture the opportunity effectively.

- **Financial Health:** Check balance sheets, debt levels, profitability, and cash flows.
- **Growth Potential:** Revenue trends, market share gains, and scalability.
- **Leadership and Governance:** Competent management, transparent practices, and strong promoter or founder commitment.
- **Competitive Advantage:** Unique products, IP, technology, or network effects that differentiate the company.

3. The Multibagger Formula in Practice

When a company with strong fundamentals operates within a sector experiencing significant tailwinds, the potential for exponential growth increases:

$$\text{Multibagger Potential} = f(\text{Sector Tailwinds} + \text{Company Fundamentals})$$

This means that a small-cap or penny stock in a rapidly growing sector, with solid financials, visionary leadership, and competitive advantages, can multiply several times its initial investment.

4. Practical Steps for Investors

1. **Identify high-growth sectors:** Use industry reports, news, and trend analysis.

2. **Screen for strong companies:** Look for financial stability, consistent revenue growth, and strong management.

3. **Evaluate tailwind sustainability:** Ensure the sector growth is not a short-term fad but has structural drivers.

4. **Combine technical and fundamental insights:** Confirm timing, market positioning, and growth momentum for optimal entry.

5. Key Takeaways

- Multibagger stocks are rarely accidental—they result from sector-driven opportunities and strong company fundamentals.

- Investing without sector tailwinds is riskier; even strong companies may struggle in stagnant industries.

- Penny stocks can deliver outsized returns if the underlying company is well-positioned to exploit structural growth trends.

By systematically combining sector tailwinds with rigorous fundamental analysis, investors can develop a repeatable framework for identifying potential multibaggers and maximize the probability of long-term wealth creation.

16.3 Applying the Multibagger Formula: Real-World Examples

Understanding theory is essential, but applying the multibagger formula in practice separates successful investors from others. In this section, we examine how sector tailwinds and company fundamentals interact in real-world penny and small-cap stocks across different markets.

1. Case Study: Artificial Intelligence (AI)

Sector Tailwind: Global AI adoption is accelerating, with enterprise AI, generative AI, and machine learning solutions experiencing exponential demand.

Company Fundamentals: Consider a small AI startup with a solid product pipeline, minimal debt, and early enterprise partnerships.

Outcome: Early investors who identified both strong fundamentals and sector tailwinds saw potential returns exceeding 10x within 2–3 years.

Lesson: Even small-cap companies can ride macro trends if they are well-managed and positioned in sectors with structural growth.

2. Case Study: Electric Vehicles (EVs)

Sector Tailwind: EVs benefit from government subsidies, environmental regulations, and rising global adoption.

Company Fundamentals: A small EV component manufacturer with innovative battery tech, consistent revenue growth, and low debt.

Outcome: With sector growth, the company experienced rapid valuation increases; early penny stock investors gained 20x returns in five years.

Lesson: Identifying upstream suppliers or niche players in high-growth sectors can generate outsized returns, sometimes even more than the sector leaders.

3. Case Study: Renewable Energy

Sector Tailwind: Global push for carbon neutrality fuels solar, wind, and energy storage companies.

Company Fundamentals: A mid-sized solar inverter company with solid cash flows and strong promoter credibility.

Outcome: Sector tailwinds combined with healthy fundamentals delivered 15x multibagger returns over four years.

Lesson: Sustainable sector tailwinds, when paired with financially disciplined companies, significantly enhance probability of success.

4. Case Study: Pharma and Healthcare

Sector Tailwind: Aging populations, new drug approvals, and expanding healthcare access create structural growth.

Company Fundamentals: Small-cap pharma company with unique drug formulations, low debt, and strong R&D pipeline.

Outcome: Investors experienced 12x–25x gains when sector tailwinds met robust fundamentals.

Lesson: Innovation-driven sectors often reward patient investors who combine long-term vision with financial diligence.

5. Key Takeaways for Applying the Formula Globally

- **Global Perspective:** Similar principles apply across India, US, Europe, and emerging markets; sector tailwinds may differ but fundamentals remain universal.
- **Small-Cap Potential:** Many multibaggers start as penny stocks; identifying them early is key.
- **Due Diligence Matters:** Never rely solely on hype; analyze balance sheets, growth metrics, and leadership quality.
- **Timing + Patience:** Entry timing and holding periods amplify returns, but patience is critical for compounding wealth.

6. Practical Steps for Investors

1. **Scan High-Growth Sectors:** Use industry reports, market news, and government policies to identify sectors with strong tailwinds.
2. **Filter Companies by Fundamentals:** Check debt levels, revenue growth, cash flows, and management credibility.
3. **Combine with Technical Insights:** Look for entry points using trendlines, support/resistance, and volume patterns.
4. **Diversify Across Sectors:** Reduce risk by holding multiple high-potential companies across complementary growth sectors.
5. **Track Progress and Adjust:** Re-evaluate sector tailwinds and company performance periodically to optimize your portfolio.

By following these steps, investors can systematically apply the multibagger formula in a global context, increasing the likelihood of turning small-cap or penny stock investments into life-changing wealth.

Key Takeaways

- **High-Growth Sectors Offer Opportunities:** Sectors such as AI, EV, Pharma, Renewable Energy, Defence, Nuclear, and Web3 are experiencing structural growth driven by technology, policy, and global demand.
- **Combine Sector Tailwinds with Fundamentals:** The most reliable multibagger opportunities arise when a company's strong financial health, management quality, and growth prospects align with favorable macro trends.

- **Small-Cap and Penny Stocks Can Lead Returns:** Early identification of companies in emerging sectors often results in outsized gains compared to mature, blue-chip stocks.
- **Global Perspective Matters:** Sector tailwinds vary by geography. India, US, Europe, and emerging markets each have unique growth drivers, so a global view enhances investment decisions.
- **Due Diligence is Critical:** Structural sector growth alone is insufficient; investors must analyze balance sheets, cash flows, debt, R&D, and management credibility to avoid pitfalls.
- **Timing and Patience Amplify Returns:** Entering early in growth sectors and holding quality companies over multiple years increases the probability of achieving multibagger returns.
- **Diversification Across Sectors Reduces Risk:** Spreading investments across multiple high-growth sectors can mitigate sector-specific downturns while maintaining upside potential.
- **Actionable Formula:** Identify sectors with strong tailwinds, filter for fundamentally solid companies, and combine with disciplined entry/exit strategies to systematically target multibagger returns.

Chapter 17

Portfolio Management & Scaling

Building a portfolio is more than simply picking high-potential penny stocks. To achieve sustainable, long-term wealth, investors must strategically combine high-risk, high-reward opportunities with stable, reliable investments in mid-cap and large-cap companies. This chapter focuses on the principles, strategies, and practical techniques for managing a diversified portfolio while scaling positions to maximize returns and control risk.
We will explore how to:

- **Blend Different Market Segments:** Learn how to integrate penny stocks, mid-caps, and large-caps to balance risk and growth potential.
- **Monitor Multibagger Potential:** Track multiple positions using metrics and analytics to identify opportunities for exponential returns while mitigating losses.
- **Implement Portfolio Rebalancing:** Understand when and how to adjust allocations to maintain optimal risk exposure, capitalize on gains, and prevent overconcentration.
- **Use Sample Allocation Tables:** Practical examples for distributing capital across different stock types and sectors, tailored to various risk appetites and investment horizons.

By the end of this chapter, readers will be equipped to construct a well-balanced, scalable portfolio that harnesses the growth potential of penny stocks while maintaining the stability of larger, more established investments. This systematic approach ensures that your portfolio is not only positioned for multibagger opportunities but also resilient to market volatility and long-term shocks.

17.1 Combining Penny Stocks with Mid-Caps and Large-Caps

Constructing a robust portfolio is not just about picking the next big winner—it is about balancing risk, reward, and stability across multiple market segments. Penny stocks, mid-caps, and large-caps each play a unique role in a diversified investment strategy, and understanding how to combine them is key to long-term wealth creation.

1. Understanding the Characteristics of Each Segment

- **Penny Stocks:** These are low-priced stocks representing early-stage companies. They have the potential for massive returns, sometimes achieving 10x or more in a short period. However, their volatility is extremely high, and liquidity can be a challenge. Penny stocks are highly sensitive to market sentiment, news, and corporate developments.
- **Mid-Cap Stocks:** Typically ranging between \$2 billion and \$10 billion in market capitalization, mid-caps offer a balance between growth potential and relative stability. They are often companies in expansion phases, benefiting from both operational momentum and increasing investor attention.
- **Large-Cap Stocks:** These are well-established companies with market capitalizations above \$10 billion. Large-caps provide stability, steady dividends, and are less prone to extreme price swings. They form the backbone of any long-term portfolio, acting as anchors during market downturns.

2. Why Combining Different Market Caps Matters

Investing across these segments allows you to harness the unique advantages of each while mitigating their respective risks:

- **Risk Diversification:** Losses in highly volatile penny stocks can be offset by the stability of large-cap holdings.
- **Growth Optimization:** Penny stocks provide exposure to explosive growth, while mid-caps capture moderate, yet significant, upward trends.
- **Portfolio Stability:** Large-caps reduce overall portfolio volatility and provide a foundation for long-term wealth.
- **Strategic Rebalancing:** With multiple segments, investors can take profits from overperforming areas and reinvest in undervalued opportunities.

3. Suggested Allocation Models

Portfolio allocation should be tailored to risk tolerance, investment horizon, and financial goals. For example:

- **Aggressive Growth:** 50% penny stocks, 30% mid-caps, 20% large-caps.
- **Balanced Approach:** 30% penny stocks, 40% mid-caps, 30% large-caps.
- **Conservative Strategy:** 10% penny stocks, 30% mid-caps, 60% large-caps.

Allocations should be revisited periodically to account for market changes, sector rotations, and portfolio performance.

4. Practical Tips for Implementation

- **Sector Diversification:** Avoid concentrating all investments in one sector to reduce risk.
- **Liquidity Management:** Ensure that penny stocks chosen are sufficiently liquid to allow easy entry and exit.
- **Research Discipline:** Use a combination of technical and fundamental analysis to identify high-potential candidates in each market segment.
- **Regular Portfolio Reviews:** Rebalance periodically to maintain your intended risk-reward profile and capture opportunities as they arise.

5. The Long-Term Perspective

While penny stocks can provide quick wins, mid-caps and large-caps ensure consistent growth and financial stability. The combined approach allows investors to ride the high-risk, high-reward nature of penny stocks without jeopardizing overall portfolio health. Over time, this strategy enhances the probability of identifying multibagger opportunities while maintaining resilience through market cycles.
By integrating penny stocks with mid-cap and large-cap investments, you create a layered portfolio that balances explosive growth potential with stability, laying a solid foundation for sustainable wealth creation and long-term financial success.

17.2 Tracking Multibagger Potential Across Multiple Positions

One of the most critical aspects of building a successful portfolio is not just selecting high-potential penny stocks or mid-cap opportunities, but actively monitoring and managing multiple positions to maximize returns. Tracking multibagger potential requires a combination of quantitative metrics, qualitative assessment, and disciplined portfolio management.

1. Understanding Multibagger Potential

A **multibagger** is an investment that grows several times over the initial investment. While past performance is not a guarantee of future returns, certain characteristics consistently indicate high potential:

- Strong revenue and earnings growth.
- Low debt and strong balance sheet.
- Innovative products, market disruption, or emerging trends.
- High insider and promoter confidence, as reflected by holdings and strategic moves.

Tracking these metrics across multiple positions ensures that you can identify which stocks are on track to deliver exponential growth.

2. Establishing Monitoring Systems

To track multibagger potential efficiently, use a combination of tools, charts, and performance metrics:

- **Portfolio Dashboard:** Maintain a centralized dashboard showing current prices, gains/losses, percentage growth, and historical performance.
- **Alerts and Notifications:** Set alerts for price movements, news, earnings reports, and volume spikes for each stock.
- **Regular Analysis:** Weekly or monthly reviews to assess performance, compare with sector benchmarks, and identify emerging opportunities.
- **Visualization Tools:** Charts tracking cumulative returns, drawdowns, and volatility help quickly assess which positions have true multibagger potential.

3. Prioritizing Positions

Not all positions in a portfolio will have the same upside. It's important to categorize and prioritize based on potential:

- **High Potential:** Stocks with strong fundamentals, technical breakout signals, and favorable sector tailwinds.
- **Moderate Potential:** Stocks with reasonable growth prospects but moderate volatility or weaker sector positioning.
- **Speculative/High-Risk:** Penny stocks or micro-caps with volatile price action; high upside but substantial downside risk.

This categorization allows you to allocate resources wisely and focus attention on positions with the greatest probability of delivering multibagger returns.

4. Using Comparative Metrics

Comparing multiple positions helps identify outperformers:

- **Price-to-Earnings (P/E) Ratio:** Compare against industry peers to spot undervalued opportunities.
- **Revenue Growth Rate:** Track consistent top-line growth relative to competitors.
- **Debt-to-Equity Ratio:** Assess financial risk across positions.
- **Relative Strength Index (RSI):** Identify overbought or oversold conditions that may indicate trend reversals.

These metrics combined with sector and market analysis create a multi-dimensional view of each position.

5. Risk-Adjusted Monitoring

High returns are often accompanied by high risk. Tracking multibagger potential must include risk assessment:

- **Volatility Tracking:** Monitor beta and historical price swings.
- **Stop-Loss Management:** Adjust stop-loss thresholds dynamically for high-volatility positions.
- **Position Sizing:** Allocate smaller portions to higher-risk stocks to prevent catastrophic portfolio losses.

6. Continuous Feedback Loop

Tracking is not a one-time activity. It's a continuous cycle:

1. Identify high-potential positions.
2. Monitor metrics, news, and price action.
3. Adjust allocation, add or exit positions based on data-driven insights.
4. Reassess multibagger potential regularly to maximize portfolio growth.

By systematically tracking multiple positions, investors can not only identify potential multibaggers early but also optimize risk-reward balance, ensuring long-term portfolio resilience and wealth creation.

17.3 Portfolio Rebalancing and Sample Allocation Tables for Long-Term Growth

Effective portfolio management goes beyond selecting high-potential penny stocks, mid-caps, and large-caps. To ensure sustained wealth creation and manage risk, regular **portfolio rebalancing** and strategic **allocation planning** are essential. This section will explain why rebalancing is critical, how to approach it, and provide sample allocation tables for long-term growth.

1. Understanding Portfolio Rebalancing

Portfolio rebalancing is the process of realigning your investments to maintain a desired risk-reward ratio. Over time, due to market movements:

- High-performing assets may become overweight, increasing portfolio risk.
- Underperforming or slow-growing assets may become underrepresented.

Rebalancing ensures that your portfolio remains aligned with your investment goals, risk tolerance, and long-term strategy.

2. Why Rebalancing Matters

- **Risk Management:** Prevents overexposure to volatile penny stocks or single sectors.
- **Disciplined Investing:** Encourages selling high and buying low, countering emotional biases.
- **Long-Term Growth:** Maintains exposure to stable mid-caps and large-caps while benefiting from multibagger potential in smaller stocks.
- **Adaptability:** Responds to changing market conditions, regulatory environments, and sectoral trends.

3. How to Rebalance Effectively

Rebalancing can be done on a time-based schedule (e.g., quarterly, bi-annually) or a threshold-based approach (when asset allocation deviates beyond a set percentage). Steps include:

1. **Assess Current Allocation:** Review your portfolio to determine actual exposure by asset class, sector, and market cap.
2. **Compare With Target Allocation:** Align current holdings with your predefined allocation strategy (e.g., 50% large-cap, 30% mid-cap, 20% penny stocks).
3. **Identify Overweight/Underweight Assets:** Determine which assets exceed or fall short of target percentages.
4. **Execute Adjustments:** Sell overweight assets and reinvest in underweight categories to restore balance.
5. **Document Changes:** Maintain records of rebalancing decisions to track performance and refine strategy.

4. Sample Allocation Tables for Long-Term Growth

While every investor's risk appetite and goals differ, here is a sample allocation strategy for a diversified portfolio targeting long-term multibagger growth:

Asset Class	**Percentage Allocation**	**Purpose**
Large-Cap Stocks	40%	Stability, lower risk, steady dividends
Mid-Cap Stocks	30%	Growth potential with moderate volatility
Penny/Small-Cap Stocks	20%	High-risk, high-reward multibagger opportunities
Bonds/Fixed Income	5%	Risk mitigation, portfolio stability
Cash/Cash Equivalents	5%	Flexibility for opportunistic buys

Table 17.1: Sample Portfolio Allocation for Long-Term Growth

This allocation can be further refined by sector exposure, geographic diversification, or specific investment themes such as AI, renewable energy, or healthcare.

5. Rebalancing in Action: Practical Tips

- **Set Thresholds:** Example: rebalance when any asset class exceeds 5% above or below target.
- **Avoid Overtrading:** Excessive buying and selling can incur fees and taxes; focus on strategic rebalancing.
- **Incorporate New Investments:** Use fresh capital to restore balance instead of only selling high.
- **Monitor Correlations:** Ensure that your portfolio isn't overly concentrated in assets that move together.
- **Adapt to Life Goals:** Adjust allocation as your risk tolerance, financial goals, and market conditions evolve.

6. Long-Term Growth Mindset

Rebalancing is not about chasing short-term gains; it is about maintaining a disciplined framework that allows your portfolio to capture growth while managing risk. By systematically monitoring allocations and making adjustments, investors can:

- Ensure sustained exposure to potential multibaggers.
- Protect against catastrophic losses in volatile markets.
- Compound wealth efficiently over years and decades.

Combining strategic allocation with careful rebalancing creates a portfolio that is resilient, growth-oriented, and positioned for long-term wealth creation.

Key Takeaways

- **Diversification is Essential:** Combining penny stocks with mid-caps and large-caps helps balance high-risk, high-reward opportunities with stable, long-term growth.
- **Monitor Multibagger Potential:** Track multiple positions systematically to identify early signs of exponential growth while managing risk exposure.
- **Rebalancing Protects Portfolio Health:** Regularly realign allocations to maintain your target risk-reward ratio and prevent overweighting volatile assets.

- **Strategic Allocation Matters:** Use sample allocation tables as a guideline to distribute capital across asset classes, sectors, and risk levels.
- **Disciplined Execution:** Combining fundamentals, technicals, and allocation discipline increases the likelihood of long-term wealth creation.
- **Adapt to Market Conditions:** Continuously assess your portfolio and adjust allocations according to market trends, sector performance, and emerging opportunities.
- **Long-Term Growth Mindset:** Scaling a portfolio is not about chasing short-term gains but about compounding returns and preserving capital over decades.

Chapter 18

Systematic Compounding

In the world of investing, small, consistent gains can accumulate into extraordinary wealth when compounded systematically over time. This chapter explores how to harness the power of compounding, combining disciplined investing with strategic decision-making to turn modest investments into life-changing financial outcomes.
We will focus on creating repeatable systems for identifying potential multibaggers, allowing you to replicate success without relying on luck. By analyzing patterns, understanding market dynamics, and leveraging both fundamentals and technical indicators, you can build a structured approach to wealth creation that works across markets and asset classes.
Importantly, this chapter also emphasizes learning from failures. Every misstep in trading and investing contains valuable lessons. By systematically reviewing what went wrong, adjusting strategies, and refining risk management practices, you can improve your overall ROI and enhance your ability to capture future opportunities.
Whether you are a beginner seeking structured guidance or an experienced trader looking to optimize returns, this chapter will equip you with the mindset, tools, and actionable systems to transform small gains into sustainable, long-term wealth.

18.1 Transforming Small Gains into Life Changing Wealth

Building wealth is rarely about sudden windfalls or lucky trades. True, lasting financial success comes from systematically turning small, consistent gains into exponential growth over time. This principle, often overlooked by beginners, is the foundation of compounding—the secret engine behind multibaggor investments and generational wealth.

1. The Power of Compounding

Compounding is the process by which your returns generate additional returns. In other words, the money you earn starts working for you, creating a snowball effect. Even modest gains, when reinvested consistently, can grow exponentially. Consider the basic formula:

$$FV = PV \times (1 + r)^n \tag{18.1}$$

Where:

- FV = Future Value of investment
- PV = Present Value or initial investment
- r = Rate of return per period
- n = Number of periods

For example, a $1,000 investment growing at 10% per quarter can exceed $14,000 in five years through disciplined reinvestment. This demonstrates how small, incremental gains—when compounded—can lead to life-changing wealth.

2. Incremental Wins Matter

Small gains are often undervalued because they don't provide immediate gratification. However, focusing on repeatable, low-risk profits reduces exposure to large losses. Each incremental win acts as a feedback loop, helping refine your investment strategy and providing confidence to scale positions responsibly.

3. Case Studies of Small Gains Turning Big

Consider an investor who earns 5–10% gains each month from carefully selected penny stocks. Over three years, consistent reinvestment of profits can transform a modest $2,000 investment into over $15,000. Historical examples from multibagger stocks in India and the U.S. show that early compounding often matters more than hitting a single "home-run" trade.

4. Strategies to Maximize Compounding

- **Reinvest Profits:** Avoid withdrawing gains too early; let your capital accumulate and grow.
- **Diversify Strategically:** Spread investments across multiple high-potential penny stocks to reduce risk while maximizing upside.
- **Focus on Probabilities:** Use fundamental and technical analysis to identify stocks with repeatable upward potential.

- **Track & Adjust:** Maintain a detailed record of performance to learn from patterns, mistakes, and successes.

5. Mindset for Long-Term Growth

Compounding requires patience, discipline, and consistency. Resist the temptation of high-risk, "get-rich-quick" strategies that promise instant wealth but often result in losses. Treat every small gain as a building block of long-term wealth creation. Over time, these small victories combine to form a robust financial foundation capable of generating life-changing returns.

6. Applying Compounding to Penny Stocks

In volatile penny stock markets, compounding can be especially powerful. By consistently reinvesting profits from small, successful trades, you can build a portfolio that grows faster than market averages. The key is to balance risk with high-potential opportunities, maintain a repeatable process, and learn from every gain or loss.

Ultimately, transforming small gains into life-changing wealth is not about luck—it's about systems, discipline, and the patient application of the compounding principle.

18.2 Repeatable Systems for Identifying Future Multibaggers

Finding multibagger stocks consistently is less about luck and more about building a structured, repeatable system. A system allows investors to identify high-potential opportunities, evaluate risk, and make informed decisions without relying on hunches or speculation.

1. Core Principles of a Repeatable System

A successful system for spotting multibaggers combines both fundamental and technical analysis while considering market dynamics:

- **Screening for Fundamentals:** Look for companies with strong balance sheets, low debt, growing revenues, and competent management.

- **Sector Tailwinds:** Focus on industries with high growth potential, such as AI, EV, renewable energy, and biotech.

- **Technical Confirmation:** Identify entry points using chart patterns, trendlines, support/resistance levels, and moving averages.

- **Risk Assessment:** Evaluate volatility, liquidity, and market manipulation potential to manage downside risk.

- **Scalability:** Ensure the system can be applied repeatedly across multiple stocks and market conditions.

2. Step-by-Step Process

A structured workflow ensures consistency and reduces emotional bias:

1. **Idea Generation:** Use screeners and news to identify penny stocks or small-cap opportunities with growth potential.
2. **Fundamental Analysis:** Assess financial health, sector growth, promoter quality, and earnings trajectory.
3. **Technical Analysis:** Look for patterns and indicators that suggest favorable entry points.
4. **Validation:** Cross-check insights with historical performance, peer comparison, and industry trends.
5. **Position Sizing:** Allocate capital proportionally based on risk tolerance and confidence level.
6. **Monitoring and Adjustment:** Track performance, set stop-loss levels, and adjust the system based on outcomes.

3. Benefits of a Repeatable System

- **Reduces Emotional Trading:** A structured process limits impulsive decisions driven by fear or greed.
- **Improves Efficiency:** Investors can quickly screen, analyze, and prioritize high-potential stocks.
- **Enhances Learning:** Each trade adds to historical data, helping refine the system and improve accuracy over time.
- **Scalability Across Markets:** Systems can be adapted for different exchanges—India, US, and emerging markets—ensuring global applicability.

4. Incorporating Feedback Loops

A system is only as good as the feedback it produces. Track successes and failures meticulously:

- Maintain a trading journal detailing entry/exit points, rationale, and outcome.

- Analyze patterns in wins and losses to adjust screening criteria and risk parameters.
- Continuously iterate the system to account for changing market conditions.

5. Practical Example

Imagine an investor using a system to evaluate small-cap tech stocks:

1. Screen for companies with revenue growth ¿30% and debt-to-equity ¡0.5.
2. Identify technical setups like breakouts from consolidation or support bounce.
3. Allocate 5–10% of portfolio per stock with predefined stop-loss and profit targets.
4. Reinvest profits into the next high-potential opportunity, compounding gains over time.

By following such a repeatable, disciplined approach, the likelihood of identifying multibagger stocks increases dramatically, while limiting emotional errors and unnecessary risk.

6. Key Takeaways

- A repeatable system blends fundamentals, technicals, and risk assessment.
- Consistency and discipline are more important than hitting occasional home runs.
- Feedback loops improve accuracy and refine strategies for future trades.
- Global applicability allows adaptation across different markets and asset classes.

18.3 Learning from Failures to Improve ROI

In the journey of investing in penny stocks, failures are inevitable. Even the most experienced investors face losses. The key difference between successful and unsuccessful traders lies in how they analyze failures, extract lessons, and refine their strategies. Learning from mistakes is not a setback—it's a critical step toward improving Return on Investment (ROI) over time.

1. Embracing a Growth Mindset

A growth mindset turns failures into opportunities for learning:

- **Accept Mistakes:** Recognize that losses are part of the learning curve, especially in volatile markets.
- **Stay Objective:** Avoid emotional reactions like blame or panic. Treat each failure as data for analysis.
- **Focus on Patterns:** Identify recurring mistakes—e.g., poor entry timing, ignoring fundamentals, over-leveraging.

2. Post-Trade Analysis

Every trade, whether successful or unsuccessful, provides valuable insights:

1. **Document the Trade:** Record entry and exit points, reasoning, technical setups, fundamental analysis, and outcome.
2. **Analyze Mistakes:** Did you ignore risk management? Did hype influence the decision? Was your analysis incomplete?
3. **Compare to Successes:** Understanding what worked in winning trades can highlight strategies worth repeating.

3. Refining Strategies

Failure-driven insights allow you to tweak your investment approach:

- Adjust position sizing to manage risk more effectively.
- Reassess stop-loss levels and exit strategies.
- Refine screening criteria to filter out low-probability stocks.
- Enhance technical analysis skills, recognizing patterns earlier and more accurately.

4. Psychological Resilience

Learning from failures strengthens emotional resilience:

- Reduces fear and anxiety associated with volatile markets.
- Prevents overreaction to short-term losses or market swings.
- Cultivates patience and discipline, crucial for multibagger investments.

5. Building a Feedback Loop

A systematic feedback loop ensures continuous improvement:

1. Review past trades weekly or monthly.
2. Categorize losses by type: strategy errors, emotional decisions, or external market factors.
3. Implement incremental changes and track the effect on ROI.
4. Repeat the cycle to progressively increase profitability and reduce avoidable mistakes.

6. Real-Life Illustration

Consider a trader who bought several small-cap stocks without thorough research, chasing hype. A month later, the stocks plummeted, resulting in significant losses. Instead of giving up:

- The trader reviewed each position, identifying the lack of fundamental analysis as the primary cause.
- He refined his screening system to include debt ratios, promoter credibility, and sector growth.
- Over the next six months, this systematic approach reduced losses and produced consistent, profitable trades.

7. Key Takeaways

- Failures are opportunities to learn and refine your investment strategy.
- Maintaining detailed trade records and performing post-mortem analyses improves decision-making.
- Continuous refinement through feedback loops increases ROI and reduces risk.
- Emotional resilience and discipline are as crucial as analytical skills for long-term success.

By embracing failures as a teacher rather than a setback, investors can transform mistakes into stepping stones, gradually building a systematic, profitable approach for identifying multibaggers and compounding wealth over time.

Key Takeaways

- **Small Gains, Big Impact:** Consistently capturing modest profits and compounding them over time can create substantial wealth, even from limited initial capital.
- **Repeatable Systems:** Developing a structured, repeatable process for identifying high-potential penny stocks increases the likelihood of finding future multibaggers.
- **Discipline and Consistency:** Following your system without letting emotions dictate decisions is critical for compounding gains effectively.
- **Learning from Failures:** Analyzing unsuccessful trades, understanding mistakes, and refining strategies improves ROI and reduces repeated errors.
- **Feedback Loops:** Regular review and adjustment of strategies ensure continuous improvement and long-term financial growth.
- **Patience and Long-Term Perspective:** Wealth through compounding and multibaggers requires time, persistence, and a focus on long-term results rather than short-term excitement.
- **Risk Management:** Protecting capital through diversification, stop-losses, and sensible position sizing ensures that compounding is sustainable and resilient to market volatility.

Part VI

Appendix

Penny Stock Master Checklist

Overview

This checklist is designed to provide a structured framework for evaluating penny stocks. It combines **fundamentals, technical analysis, and risk filters** to help traders and investors identify high-potential opportunities while minimizing exposure to pitfalls.

1. Fundamental Checklist

- **Financial Health:**
  - Positive revenue growth over 2-3 years
  - Low or manageable debt levels
  - Healthy cash flow and liquidity ratios
- **Promoter and Insider Holdings:**
  - High promoter stake indicates commitment
  - Track insider buying/selling activity
  - Avoid stocks with frequent promoter pledging
- **Earnings and Profitability:**
  - Consistent EPS growth
  - Reasonable profit margins for the sector
  - Dividend history (if applicable)
- **Sector and Market Potential:**
  - Growing industry tailwinds (AI, EV, Pharma, Renewable, etc.)
  - Competitive positioning and innovation
  - Regulatory clarity and market opportunity

2. Technical Analysis Checklist

- **Trend Analysis:**
  - Check long-term trend direction
  - Moving averages (50 EMA, 200 EMA) alignment
  - Trendlines for support/resistance
- **Price Patterns:**
  - Identify breakout, consolidation, triangle, flag patterns
  - Look for double tops/bottoms and reversal signals
  - Use mini charts for visual confirmation
- **Volume and Momentum Indicators:**
  - Rising volume confirms strength
  - RSI, MACD, and stochastic indicators for momentum
  - Pre-market and after-hours activity tracking

3. Risk Filters Checklist

- **Volatility Assessment:**
  - Average daily price swings
  - Liquidity levels to avoid thinly traded traps
- **Scam and Manipulation Risks:**
  - Avoid pump-and-dump schemes
  - Track social media hype critically
  - Verify news from official sources
- **Position Sizing and Diversification:**
  - Allocate only a portion of capital per penny stock
  - Maintain a diversified portfolio of 5–10 high-potential stocks

    Apply stop loss limits and exit plans

4. Action Plan

1. Shortlist stocks that pass all fundamental checks
2. Apply technical analysis for entry timing
3. Apply risk filters before committing capital
4. Document your decisions and review outcomes regularly
5. Adjust your checklist and strategy based on lessons learned

Tip: Use this checklist as a repeatable system. Consistency in applying these filters will improve your probability of identifying high-potential multibagger penny stocks while minimizing avoidable risks.

Glossary

Overview

This glossary is intended to provide clear and concise definitions of the most commonly used terms in penny stock trading, investing, and market analysis. Understanding these terms is crucial for both beginners and experienced investors to navigate markets confidently.

A

- **Accumulation:** The phase in which smart money or institutional investors gradually buy shares without significantly affecting the price.
- **ADR (American Depository Receipt):** A negotiable certificate representing shares in a foreign company traded on U.S. exchanges.

B

- **Bid Price:** The highest price a buyer is willing to pay for a stock at a given moment.
- **Blue-Chip Stocks:** Shares of large, well-established, financially sound companies known for stability and dividends.
- **Breakout:** When a stock price moves above a resistance level or below a support level, often signaling the start of a new trend.

C

- **Candlestick Chart:** A type of chart that displays open, high, low, and close prices for a stock within a specific time period.
- **Circuit Breaker:** A regulatory measure to temporarily halt trading on an exchange to curb panic-selling.

- **Consolidation:** A period when a stock trades within a range, showing indecision between buyers and sellers before the next trend.

D

- **Day Trading:** Buying and selling securities within the same trading day to take advantage of intraday price movements.
- **Debt-Free Company:** A company with little or no long-term liabilities, often considered less risky for investment.

E

- **Earnings Per Share (EPS):** The portion of a company's profit allocated to each outstanding share of common stock.
- **Ex-Dividend Date:** The date on which a stock begins trading without the value of its next dividend payment.

F

- **FOMO (Fear of Missing Out):** Emotional reaction that drives investors to buy a stock due to hype or rapid price increases.
- **Fundamental Analysis:** Evaluating a company's financial statements, sector, and growth potential to estimate its intrinsic value.

H

- **Head and Shoulders:** A reversal chart pattern signaling a potential change in trend direction.

I

- **Insider Trading:** Buying or selling a company's stock based on material, non-public information. Legal only if disclosed and compliant with regulations.

L

- **Liquidity:** The ease with which a stock can be bought or sold without affecting its price.

M

- **Multibagger:** A stock that generates returns multiple times its original investment, e.g., 5x, 10x, or more.
- **Momentum Trading:** A strategy of buying stocks that show upward price trends and selling those with downward trends.

O

- **Over-The-Counter (OTC) Markets:** Decentralized markets where stocks not listed on formal exchanges are traded.

P

- **Penny Stock:** A low-priced, small-cap stock often trading under $5 (USD) or equivalent in other currencies. Highly volatile but with potential for high returns.
- **Promoter Holdings:** The percentage of shares owned by the original founders or key stakeholders.

R

- **Resistance Level:** A price point at which a stock faces selling pressure, preventing further upward movement.
- **Risk Management:** Strategies to limit potential losses through diversification, position sizing, stop-loss orders, and other techniques.

S

- **Support Level:** A price point where a stock tends to find buying interest, preventing further decline.
- **Swing Trading:** Trading strategy focusing on short- to medium-term price movements, typically a few days to weeks.

V

- **Volatility:** The degree of variation in a stock's price over time; higher volatility implies higher risk and potential reward.

W

- **Volume:** The total number of shares traded during a specific period, used to confirm trends and breakouts.

Conclusion

A solid understanding of these terms is essential for anyone navigating the penny stock market. This glossary serves as a reference guide to reinforce your learning from fundamentals, technicals, and real-life trading experiences. Keep revisiting it to strengthen your command of penny stock investing language.

Resources: Global Tools, Apps, Websites, Newsletters, YouTube Channels, and Recommended Books

Overview

Successful investing in penny stocks and small-cap opportunities requires reliable tools, accurate data, and continuous learning. This chapter provides a curated, global set of resources to help investors screen, analyze, and track high-potential stocks while minimizing risks. Resources include apps, websites, newsletters, YouTube channels, and books, with guidance for both beginners and advanced traders.

Global Apps and Trading Platforms

Stock Trading Platforms

These platforms allow buying, selling, and monitoring stocks across regions:

- **Robinhood (US/Global)**: Commission-free trades, beginner-friendly, real-time market data.
- **Webull (US/Global)**: Advanced charts, screening tools, paper trading.
- **Fidelity / TD Ameritrade / Charles Schwab (US)**: Robust research, retirement accounts, international stocks.
- **Trading 212 (Europe/Global)**: Stocks, ETFs, fractional shares, beginner-friendly interface.

- **Interactive Brokers (Global)**: Professional-grade platform, low-cost international trading, advanced analytics.
- **Groww, Zerodha, Angel One (India)**: Local market access, low brokerage, beginner-friendly tools.

Charting and Technical Analysis Apps

For research, screening, and pattern recognition:

- **TradingView**: Global charts, technical indicators, alerts, and community ideas.
- **Finviz (US)**: Visual stock screening, heat maps, penny stock filters.
- **Screener.in (India)**: Fundamental analysis and filters for Indian markets.
- **StockCharts.com**: Technical charting and indicators for global stocks.
- **Yahoo Finance / Google Finance**: Quick reference for real-time prices and financial news.

Mobile vs Desktop

- **Mobile apps**: Convenient for intraday tracking, alerts, and basic trades.
- **Desktop platforms**: Essential for deep technical analysis, screening, portfolio management, and backtesting.
- Recommendation: Use mobile apps for alerts and monitoring, desktop platforms for research and execution.

Global Websites and News Sources

Stay updated with accurate information for timing trades and understanding market sentiment:

- **Bloomberg, Reuters, CNBC, Financial Times**: Global financial news and market trends.
- **Investing.com**: Real-time global market data, economic calendars, and technical analysis.
- **Moneycontrol / Economic Times Markets (India)**: Local market news, corporate results, and stock analysis.
- **MarketWatch / Nasdaq / NYSE official sites**: US-focused corporate filings and stock data.

- **EDGAR (SEC filings)**: Official financial statements for US-listed companies.

Newsletters and Email Alerts

Subscribe to expert analysis and curated stock ideas:

- **Motley Fool Stock Advisor**: Long-term growth recommendations.
- **Morningstar Premium**: Fundamental analysis and valuation insights.
- **SmallCapWorld / Microcap Confidential**: Specialized newsletters for penny and small-cap stocks.
- **Investopedia Newsletter**: Educational updates and market insights.
- **Seeking Alpha Alerts**: Community-driven analysis and earnings commentary.

YouTube Channels

Video-based learning, tutorials, and real-time analysis:

- **Financial Education (Jeremy Lefebvre)**: Growth and small-cap investing insights.
- **Trader University / Rayner Teo**: Technical analysis and trading strategies.
- **Rachit Jain / MarketGurukul / Finology** (India): Indian market penny stock tutorials.
- **Bloomberg QuickTake / CNBC Television**: Global market news and analysis.

Filter and Screening Tools

Use these tools to shortlist stocks before investing:

- Filter by price, volume, debt-free status, promoter holdings, and sector.
- Apply technical indicators: RSI, moving averages, and MACD to confirm trends.
- Use multi-factor screening to reduce false positives and minimize risk.

Recommended Books

Develop foundational knowledge, risk management skills, and market psychology:

- **The Intelligent Investor** by Benjamin Graham – Value investing principles.
- **Common Stocks and Uncommon Profits** by Philip Fisher – Growth investing framework.
- **One Up on Wall Street** by Peter Lynch – Identifying multibagger stocks early.
- **How to Make Money in Stocks** by William O'Neil – Technical analysis and CAN SLIM strategy.
- **Market Wizards** by Jack D. Schwager – Trader psychology and success stories.
- **The Little Book That Still Beats the Market** by Joel Greenblatt – Quantitative investing approach.

Conclusion

By integrating global apps, platforms, websites, newsletters, YouTube tutorials, and books, investors can create a comprehensive ecosystem for penny stock analysis. Combining tools with disciplined research, risk management, and practical learning helps identify multibagger opportunities while minimizing risk. Always validate information across multiple sources, and supplement digital resources with hands-on experience.

FAQs: Penny Stocks, Multibaggers, and Wealth Creation

1. Which Penny Stocks Should I Buy Now?

Penny stocks are highly volatile and carry substantial risk. Rather than chasing "hot tips," focus on a systematic approach:

- **Screen using fundamentals:** Look for companies with low debt, strong promoter holdings, and growing revenues.
- **Use technical filters:** Identify stocks showing consolidation patterns, breakouts, or trend reversals.
- **Sector selection:** Emerging industries like AI, EV, renewable energy, and biotech often present higher growth potential.
- **Avoid hype-driven picks:** Social media tips or sudden spikes can lead to pump-and-dump traps.
- **Diversify:** Allocate small amounts to multiple candidates rather than betting everything on one stock.

Takeaway: There is no "guaranteed winner." Focus on structured research, risk management, and pattern recognition to identify potential candidates.

2. Can Penny Stocks Make You Rich?

Yes—but only if approached systematically and with realistic expectations:

- **Potential for multibaggers:** Small-cap and penny stocks sometimes deliver 10x, 20x, or even 50x returns, but the success rate is low.

- **High risk:** Losses are equally probable. Many penny stocks fail or stagnate due to poor fundamentals or market manipulation.
- **Compounding approach:** Gradually reinvesting profits, following disciplined strategies, and managing risk can create long-term wealth.
- **Long-term perspective:** Treat penny stocks as part of a diversified portfolio that includes mid-cap and blue-chip holdings.

Takeaway: Penny stocks can be wealth multipliers, but they are not a shortcut to riches. Knowledge, discipline, and patience are critical.

3. How Do I Spot Future Multibaggers?

Identifying potential multibaggers requires combining quantitative analysis with qualitative insight:

1. **Fundamental analysis:** Look at revenue growth, low debt, promoter holdings, and earnings consistency.
2. **Technical analysis:** Identify breakout patterns, consolidation formations, and momentum indicators.
3. **Sector tailwinds:** Target industries with long-term growth drivers like AI, EV, renewable energy, or biotech.
4. **Market sentiment:** Monitor news, regulatory changes, and earnings reports, but avoid hype-driven decisions.
5. **Diversification & scaling:** Start with small allocations, track performance, and gradually scale winners.

Takeaway: Future multibaggers are identified through disciplined research, a structured process, and consistent review, not by following tips or short-term trends.

4. Additional Practical Tips

- Keep a journal of every trade—record entry, exit, reason, and outcome.
- Regularly review your portfolio and adapt strategies based on performance.
- Treat losses as learning opportunities; avoid emotional decisions driven by fear, greed, or FOMO.
- Always use stop-loss orders and manage exposure per stock to limit downside risk.

Conclusion

Penny stocks present both opportunity and risk. By following systematic screening, analysis, risk management, and continuous learning, you can increase your probability of spotting multibagger opportunities while minimizing potential losses. The key is discipline, patience, and building a repeatable system—turning small, calculated bets into long-term wealth creation.

Exercises & Templates: Build Your Own Penny-to-Multibagger Roadmap

Overview

Turning small investments into multibagger returns requires structured planning, disciplined execution, and consistent learning. This chapter provides practical exercises and templates to help you systematically identify, track, and grow potential penny stock investments. By completing these exercises, you will create a personalized roadmap that guides you from small gains to life-changing wealth.

Exercise 1: Setting Investment Goals

Objective: Define your short-term, mid-term, and long-term financial goals.

- Short-term (1–6 months): e.g., \$100 → \$500 gains.
- Mid-term (6–24 months): e.g., \$1,000 → \$5,000 portfolio growth.
- Long-term (2–5 years+): Build a multibagger portfolio aiming for 10x–50x potential.

Goal	Timeframe	Target Returns
Short-term	6 months	\$500
Mid-term	18 months	\$5,000
Long-term	5 years	\$50,000+

Exercise 2: Stock Screening Checklist

Objective: Identify high-potential penny stocks based on fundamentals and technicals.

- Price range: \$0.10 – \$5 / INR 5 – 50
- Debt-free or manageable debt levels
- Strong promoter or management holdings
- Sector growth potential (AI, EV, Pharma, Renewables, etc.)
- Technical breakout patterns: consolidation, triangles, flags

Stock	Price	Sector	Debt Status	Technical Signal

Exercise 3: Risk Management Plan

Objective: Define your entry, exit, and stop-loss levels for each stock.

- Maximum allocation per stock: 5–10% of total portfolio
- Stop-loss: 5–15% below entry price (adjust based on volatility)
- Target exits: 2x, 5x, 10x returns (flexible)

Stock	Entry Price	Stop-Loss	Target Price

Exercise 4: Portfolio Tracking Log

Objective: Monitor portfolio performance and make data-driven decisions.

- Track daily/weekly price movements
- Record news, earnings, and events affecting stock
- Update target prices and stop-loss as trends evolve

Stock	Current Price	% Change	News/Events	Notes

Exercise 5: Weekly Review and Strategy Refinement

Objective: Reflect on trades, learn from mistakes, and optimize your approach.

- Review winning and losing trades
- Identify recurring patterns of success and failure
- Adjust screening criteria and risk management rules
- Plan the next week's trades with updated insights

Exercise 6: Multibagger Roadmap Template

Objective: Visualize your journey from small investments to potential multibaggers.

- Step 1: Start small, identify 3–5 potential penny stocks
- Step 2: Apply fundamental + technical screening
- Step 3: Allocate small capital with stop-loss
- Step 4: Track and refine weekly
- Step 5: Gradually scale winners into mid-caps and long-term holdings
- Step 6: Repeat systematically, reinvest gains, build generational wealth

Step	Action	Target	Notes	Status
1	Screen stocks	3–5 candidates		
2	Analyze fundamentals	Strong balance sheet		
3	Allocate capital	5–10% per stock		
4	Track	Weekly updates		
5	Scale winners	Mid-caps/long-term		
6	Repeat	Compounding system		

Conclusion

By completing these exercises and using the templates consistently, you create a disciplined, repeatable framework for identifying and managing potential multibagger penny stocks. The combination of goal-setting, screening, risk management, tracking, and iterative learning forms the backbone of a systematic approach to building life-changing wealth from small investments.

www.ingramcontent.com/pod-product-compliance
Ingram Content Group UK Ltd.
Pitfield, Milton Keynes, MK11 3LW, UK
UKHW020159290926
15471UKWH00005B/968

9 789334 456295